Looking Back on the Future

Timeless Wisdom of the Andes as a Bridge into the New Era

Looking Back on the Future

Timeless Wisdom of the Andes as a Bridge into the New Era

Chandra Sun Eagle

MOON BOOKS

Winchester, UK
Washington, USA

JOHN HUNT PUBLISHING

First published by Moon Books, 2021
Moon Books is an imprint of John Hunt Publishing Ltd., No. 3 East Street, Alresford
Hampshire SO24 9EE, UK
office@jhpbooks.net
www.johnhuntpublishing.com
www.moon-books.net

For distributor details and how to order please visit the 'Ordering' section on our website.

Text copyright: Chandra Sun Eagle 2020

ISBN: 978 1 78904 658 8
978 1 78904 659 5 (ebook)
Library of Congress Control Number: 2020939165

A CIP catalogue record for this book is available from the British Library.

Design: Stuart Davies

UK: Printed and bound by CPI Group (UK) Ltd, Croydon, CR0 4YY
Printed in North America by CPI GPS partners

We operate a distinctive and ethical publishing philosophy in all areas of our business, from our global network of authors to production and worldwide distribution.

Contents

In Dedication

It is with sincere and deep gratitude that I dedicate this book to the mystics, visionaries, native elders and wisdom keepers around the world who have continued to preserve the ancient teachings and shamanic traditions of the earth. It is through your ceremonies, rituals and heart centered living, that you have kept the very fabric of life alive and animated. In special honor of the Q'ero Nation, and other indigenous people of the Peruvian Andes, I thank you for sharing your sacred knowledge with such generosity and openness. I have so many teachers in North America and South America to thank for the love, support and encouragement you've offered along my path. You are my teachers in the healing arts and the world of shamanism, who helped me remember who I am and why I am here. You are the ancestors and spirits who come in my dreamtime and circle my fires. You are the nature spirits that dwell in the tree tops, the rivers and stones, the winged ones who soar through the skies, the ocean dwellers who have inhabited the waters of Mother Earth for millions of years, and you are the star beings who continually remind me from where I have come and where I will return.

Thank you Cecilia, of the Chumash Tribe, for our brief, yet potent time together. For my life changing Vision Quest, I bow in gratitude to the two sisters, Donna and Julie of the Lakota Tradition, for preparing and guiding me. For the unparalleled teachings of Dorothy, thank you. Your combined knowledge of Huna, psychology, physics, the body, nature, chemistry, and science, is beyond anyone I've ever met. To my teachers and friends in the Andes, Tito La Rosa, Don Victor Estrada, Vilma Pineda, Wilson Pineda, Karen Urcia, Jesus Casteneda, Javier Regueiro, I am eternally grateful to you all, for the connection we share, the teachings and the heart path we walk together. To

Alberto Villoldo, Ph.D, thank you for being amongst the first to recognize the medicine woman within me and for giving me a strong push to continue my journey. To John Hunt, thank you for reaching out to me, back in 2006, and providing the first breath of inspiration to write this book. Gratitude to all my friends and family, who over the years have listened and been present as I struggled with the writing process. And most of all, to my sweet and remarkable family, Aimee, Bella, and Nalu. You bring so much joy, playfulness and meaning to my life. I love you and am forever grateful for all your support. Thank you All!

Introduction

Over the years, while working for Spirit, I have learned that I will rarely get the full picture of the task or project, and that things can shift in a heartbeat; testing my trust, my aptitude to listen, my ability to stay present and willingness to be flexible. I've gotten comfortable with not knowing, and I have released the need to "know" the full scope of what's to come before entering into agreements with Spirit. It wasn't always like this, but after many years of practice, this has become a large part of the beauty and adventure of my life, the magic of my life, and expresses my fullest participation with the "The Great Mystery". I have also learned over the years that answering the call of Spirit and entering the unknown are exceptional moments of opportunity that hold the greatest potential for growth. This includes our own growth and the growth of all the people we touch along the way. We get pushed to our edges, beyond the barriers of our limitations, that we may not have even known existed. I've come to understand that certain requests from Spirit are meant to empower us, to give us courage and to teach us how to surrender to the natural flow of life and a higher power. When I answered the call of the shamanic life and path of service, my life picked up an exciting, and at times, intimidating momentum that was out of my control. I've always had a strong will, verging on stubborn, so learning to let go and shed parts of myself and aspects of my identity, in order that the new me could come through, was not always easy or comfortable. The transformation of old beliefs and an outdated self-image required daily discipline. Thankfully, my desire to overcome my obstinate position, to discover the meaning of a deep longing I felt inside, and to live my soul purpose was heard by Spirit. At the time my prayer was strong, but I honestly had no idea that my life's purpose was in the shamanic realms and would entail becoming a ceremonial leader, a carrier of plant medicine and ancient wisdom. At the time I prayed for understanding of what I was longing for, but I didn't know what it was. I only knew I hadn't found it yet.

In the late 90's I found myself experiencing life "outside the box" and outside the consensual reality lived by most. My appetite for spending time in the Mystery and in unknown realms was insatiable. The idea of who I was began to change and my relationship to the natural world took on new meaning. I had always loved the outdoors and adventure, but that love became saturated with a determination to commune on a deeper level with the Natural World and to attain spiritual wisdom from the Elements, the spirit world and the unseen realms. There were periods when my dream life seemed more real than the waking reality I was walking in. During the night I would enter other dimensions and other landscapes where I was reliving shamanic initiations I had undergone in previous lifetimes. It was all so familiar and yet so foreign to the world I was living in. Regular visitations from spirit guides and Light Beings became the norm, imparting their knowledge or running their hands over my body to clear out old energy. Each time I faced a challenge in my day-to-day waking life, it was common for memories of a time past to bleed through into my present awareness, body and dreams, sometimes leaving their mark in the morning. One morning, during a time of cultivating courage to speak my truth, I woke from having fought with a jaguar, and found a shallow gash on face and a small trickle of blood running down my cheek. The wound took only a day to heal, but left a scar for a month to follow, reminding me of the Jaguar medicine within and to stay on course. Other times my bones ached terribly, and fatigue overwhelmed my system from the mere act of dreaming. Dreaming, I came to learn for the shaman, is not always just dreaming. It is a potent and powerful time of awakening, initiation and training. About three years into my shamanic training, women clothed in green vines with multi-colored flowers, whispering "WRITE IT DOWN", began to flood my dreams on a nightly basis. Journaling was not a practice I had adopted and had actually become rather resistant to. Communicating what I was going through seemed a great challenge, and rarely, what came out on paper, captured the depth of what I was experiencing and the essence of what I felt. It was often a struggle to find the right words and to put them in a semblance that made sense. This was a great source of frustration for me, so I had left the act of journaling to those who were "writers" and found enjoyment in it. Not wanting to expose the sacredness of my inner world had become a very good reason to justify my resistance. I had also convinced myself that I would always remember every detail of the past years of my life, as the events, mystical experiences and dreams were too powerful to forget. "The stories are etched in soul, in my heart," I told myself. But the dreams kept coming, the women dressed in vines kept coming, and it became obvious that I was ignoring a very important message. So I started to write. I recorded what I was living, dreaming and what came through during journeys and meditations. I wrote about my adventures into the world of the shaman, treks through the Andes of Peru, receiving rites of passage and learning the art of energy medicine. Sometimes it was only images or symbols that I could remember from the dreamtime, and to this day I do not understand all of them. Certain dreams still linger in the pages of my journals and in my mind, returning every so often to remind me of their presence and test my ability to interpret their meaning. Who were these women wearing the dress of Mother Nature and speaking with such perseverance?

In 2005 another very unexpected call from Spirit came through the airwaves of my life. I was preparing notes for a talk and a workshop I was to give at the Sun Valley Wellness Festival, when the phone rang. The incoming call was from one of the festival's administrators asking me how much time they should allow for my book signing after my talk. After a brief but rather confusing conversation, I assured them that I was not an author and I did not have a published book. "That was odd," I thought to myself once we hung up, but I let it go and went about preparing my notes. Two days later, while finishing with preparation notes, I noticed an incoming email with a subject line entitled, "Book Inquiry". The email was from an English publishing company called O Books. With peaked curiosity, I clicked on the open tab to find that John Hunt, the founder and CEO, was writing directly to ask if I would be interested in writing a book on Peruvian Shamanism and energy medicine. John explained that he came across my web-site while searching for Andean Mysticism and after reading my bio, felt strongly to ask if I would consider writing a book for them. Quite perplexed, I stared at the email in disbelief. At the time my website was called Zen Adventures and it only had a brief explanation of my studies in Andean Spirituality. For several days I pondered the proposal that was before me. I truly was not interested in writing a book, had never considered writing a book and by no means did I feel I was studied or experienced enough at the time to take on such a task. Back and forth, I argued with myself and with Spirit. Feeling slightly tortured by the request, I knew I could not say no, but I also didn't know how to say yes. As I asked the question, "Why me?" a flash of one of the first teachings I received, struck like a lightning bolt. Alberto's voice boomed in my ears as if he was standing right next to me, "As shamans we enter into an agreement with Spirit. The agreement states that when we call upon Spirit, Spirit comes. The flip side of the agreement, the *ayni* or reciprocity, is that when Spirit calls us, we must answer." Alberto went on to explain, "For most of you, the calling on Spirit and receiving help will be the easy part. It will be answering Spirit's call that will present the challenge. At times the request will seem a great inconvenience to your life.

What will be asked of you might not be what you were planning, perhaps the timing won't be good, and maybe just maybe the service you will be asked to do will take you way out of your comfort zone, presenting challenges that seem insurmountable." "Sometimes," he went on to say, "we become complacent and lazy in our lives and just want to stay there." I have found all of this to be true on certain levels, in different moments in my life, and so, as I took to heart the resurgence of these teachings, I surrendered my points of argument, and an instant ease washed over me.

If writing a book truly was Spirit calling then I was ready to say yes. I responded to John with a, "Yes, but in six weeks I'll be back in Peru and I would like see what the Paqos (Andean medicine people) have to say about this." John said, "Certainly. Contact me when you get back." A month and half later I found myself in the Urubamba Valley, the Sacred Valley of the Inca, preparing for a two week pilgrimage to Apu Ausanagate and Apu Q'ollorit'i, two of the holy mountains and places of power that the Andean Shamans source from. It was at the base of Ausangate that I planned to ask for a coca leaf reading and the consultation of the Ancestors. The reading of coca leaves is the ancient method of divination in the Andes. My intuition told me this was the best way to confirm if I was to share what I had learned from these beautiful people and my understanding of them as I integrated the teachings into my life. Well, the reading didn't happen. I never even got the chance to ask for one. Every time I went to ask one of the paqos, I was interrupted by someone or something and was diverted away. After the third attempt I took it as a sign and decided that if reading was to happen it would. After the mountain journeys I spent a couple of days in Cusco with a good friend before departing for the Amazon to work with Ayahuasca, known as the Vine of the Soul, (an intensely beautiful experience that I share later in the book). After the Amazon and prior to coming back to the states my friend and I were taking a few more days in Cusco to relax and integrate, when the phone rang.

"Hola, Ms. Porter, this is the front desk. Adolpho and Adrian, two paqos are here to see you. They would like to come to your room." Adolpho and Adrian were the two paqos that led the Ausangate and Q'ollorit'i mountain journeys. "What are they doing here and how did they know where I was staying?" I thought to myself. "Yes, please, have them come up." I responded.

What ensued next was mind bending. I greeted the two men and invited them to come in. With only a few words they laid out their mesas (altars), sacred clothes and coca leaves, and then told me they were here to do my reading. Astounded at the turn of events, I placed my mesa at the altar of Mama Coca, and said I wished to see what the leaves had to say without me asking any questions. The first throw of the leaves revealed good news about my healing work and my upcoming move to Kauai, HI. It was the second throw of leaves that grabbed all of our attention, when Adrienne pointed to a cluster of several leaves that had landed perfectly, one on top of the other. Speaking with excitement, Adrienne spoke what he saw in the arrangement of leaves, "You are to write a book. The book is to be about the Andean spiritual tradition. It will go everywhere." And then they both looked at me with a gleam of blessing. There it was, the confirmation I was seeking.

And so, 15 years and several versions later, here is my offering to Spirit's request.

The Invitation

There is a great cosmic invitation being extended to all the Children of the Earth at this time. It is a calling to participate consciously with the magic and mystery of the Universe as we pass through this phase of collective and global purification, and into a new phase of creation, known in the Andean Tradition as the Taripay Pacha; A Golden Age of Encounter, of Meeting Ourselves Again. The wisdom keepers and mystics of the Peruvian Andes refer to The Golden Age as a time in which we will encounter the true and authentic aspects of our Spiritual Nature and our Oneness with all Life. They speak of our co-creative powers and higher wisdom being buried deep within the rubble of karmic accumulation and crystalized layers of energetic imprinting of the past, held not only in our energy bodies and psyches, but in the energy field of the Earth as well.

We are in the midst of a massive shift on planet Earth. The stars are singing to each of us, transmitting a signal that carries with it the celestial signature of our Over Soul and our High Self. The rise of a New Humanity is encouraging us each to illuminate the unconscious, to shed the old and rediscover our Origins. It is a time in which to call forth from the distant past, the memory of a pristine Earth and spiritually evolved humanity, where peace, integrity, balance, respect, love and spiritual love reigned through the people and land. Perhaps some have forgotten the Divine origins from which they come, but this does not mean they have been forgotten. Through the Central Sun, the Light of Creator is sending waves of Liquid Truth Light and Love, beckoning us all to step back into the River of Life, and to re-orient ourselves with the sacred and natural laws of creation, as well as our purpose within creation.

I have experienced and continue to experience this cosmic invitation as a call to return Home, as my Soul's journey back into unity consciousness, wholeness and harmonious communion with Creator. I'd like to invite you to answer the call of this invitation. Grant yourself the permission to follow your soul's impulse to return to union with the Heart of Creation and re-union with your own sacred nature. Through remembering your authentic essence, your Divinity and your interconnectedness with all Life you are answering the call of creation and the call of your individual soul and the Soul of the Collective. There is no greater calling. Upon accepting the invitation, an epic voyage of the soul commences and your spiritual evolution will sprout new wings for an expedition of Universal flight that offers liberation from karmic ties, ancestral and societal restrictions, false education, limitations and bondages of fear. The adventure is a sojourn of remembering your original essence, your divinity and your interconnectedness with all life. It is a retrieval of and a reconnection with lost or forgotten soul parts and your Star Seed lineage. The journey is also a wild exploration, recovery and healing of the past that bestows many gifts upon the seeker. It is a great journey that requires the balance of discipline with spontaneity, the courage to change and the courage to soar with an open heart. The path to wholeness and liberation requires acceptance, humility, forgiveness and surrender, the ability to find stillness and the ability to flow. Answering the call is a courageous act of surrender and willingness to drop what we think we know, to re-examine the manual of man-made law in order to re-align with the Essence of Spirit and Universal Law. The path is not always clear, nor is it always comfortable, and so ensues the training of a true Light Warrior. Our encounters and experiences along the way are perhaps different, but at a core level of our soul, there are many shared commonalities to what we seek. We all seek peace, to experience a joyful life, to love and to be Loved. We all seek to experience life beyond the limitations of fear and lack and to live with creative expression, abundance and purpose. Our souls yearn to understand our place in the world and to be part of something greater than our individual self, while living a life filled with meaning. The Wisdom of the Andean Mystics, along with other Indigenous Wisdom Keepers around the world, provide us with a map for this epic voyage.

Many times, I have been told by teachers, and have heard through the channeling of the stars, that this lifetime, more than learning new things, is a lifetime to remember. A lifetime to remember all that we know and all that we are. In this lifetime we have come to master the evolutionary process and be able to live in and with our full potential, functioning in many realities. In the living of our full potential we are able to transmute the denser energies of past experiences, although necessary for our growth, that have become a burden on our souls and the earth. As we transform and remember our wholeness an alignment with the natural evolution of the Earth and the divine unfolding of creation occurs. As we transmute the denser energies, we join the cosmic flow and dimensional shift that is happening on the earth. It is a great opportunity we have before us. An opportunity to make a shift into higher frequencies of Love, harmony and the sacred realities of creation. As this shift occurs our luminous energy field reorganizes itself to reflect the totality of a healed and whole state. An energetic state that at its core is a cosmic seed of Divine Consciousness, burning with the fire and passion of our Creator. With our hearts open, our roots grow deeper and our branches higher. As we make the shift into higher frequencies of compassion, reverence and respect, we go through a bio-chemical process that turns us to gold, shining like the Sun and radiating these frequencies down into the earth and out into stars. And in doing so we become true Children of the Sun. We become what we are and who we are meant to be, bridges between the Earth and Sky, Spirit and Matter, the seen and unseen, the form and the formless.

Throughout my travels and studies, I've had the honor to sit with and to learn from great medicine people of North

America and different regions of South America. It has been the culmination of the Andean mystics and shamans of Peru, their living and non-living lineage, their energetic transmissions and wisdom teachings, that makes up the majority of my training and the energy medicine I use today in ritual, ceremony and healing. Of the energetic transmissions and wisdom teachings I've received, what struck me most as key elements to share in this book, are from the Q'ero people and are referred to as the 7 *Saiwas*, or the 7 Universal Laws that lead to the transformation of consciousness and reconnection with Source. This body of Organic Cosmic Law has been a foundational map of inquiry and guidance along my path of awakening. I'll also share with you pieces of my personal journey that are relevant to the 7 Saiwas, as well as some of the nature based, ritual and energetic practices that I have learned and developed along the way. The 7 Saiwas have been foundational for my journey and path to becoming a person of wisdom, power and grace. They have been essential for cleaning out the cob-webs of my subconscious, re-wiring neural pathways and my Luminous Energy Field and learning to become a conscious dreamer and weaver of creation. Upon receiving this spiritual body of wisdom, I instantly knew the 7 Saiwas were gems to be shared with the world. I felt a knowing inside that the 7 Saiwas, and the teachings that lead to an understanding and embodiment of these laws, could be very helpful, if not essential, in our collective awakening. My prayer is that your life become more peaceful, joyful and connected as a result of learning and putting into practice this Universal wisdom. May you find what you need for taking the next step in your soul's evolution. May you learn ways to manage your own energy field and techniques for self-healing as you travel the spiral of ascension. May you learn to balance and master your emotions, honor your body and master your mind and its unlimited potential for creation. May you become a magnificent creator, a server of Light, and a great caretaker of our Mother

Earth and all our relations. May you align your inner self and outer life with the coming of the *"Golden Age."*

Wisdom Descending - A prophecy coming to pass

In the early to mid-1980's a few of the last of the Inca descendants, known as the Q'ero nation, who unknown to the world, had survived the Spanish Inquisition, began descending from their homes high in the Andes. No one knew any of these tribe members had survived the Spanish invasion. Entire villages of people high in the Andes at over 14,000 feet, 500 years after the Spanish Inquisition, isolated from the modern world, lived the purity of their traditions and ceremonial lives in alignment with cosmic knowledge. These beautiful wisdom keepers of the sacred continued to live and preserve an ancient body of knowledge, energetic transmissions and prophecy. The Q'ero knew that it was time for their return. As Children of the Sun and masters of the world of energy, it was recorded in their oral history that the day would come when the children of the world would be ready for their teachings and be ready to assist with the birth of a new era of peace. And so, they walked out of their stone walled, thatched roof dwellings, out of their potato fields and Alpaca flocks and into an unknown, chaotic, modern world, carrying within them some of the purest and most relevant energy of our times. They invite us to walk the Qapac Nan - The Royal Road and Spiritual Path of consciousness, respect and reverence for the living world, while tending to the garden of our life, pulling out the weeds and planting more seeds of Love, while watering, nourishing and restoring balance to our spiritual growth.

It was "written" in their prophecy and thus it was time. Part of this prophecy speaks of a 500-year period of spiritual darkness on earth when fear, war and chaos would reign. The ways of the feminine would be forgotten and the rivers and oceans would become polluted. However, at the end of this 500 years, the Condor of South America and the Eagle of North America would fly wing to wing once again, symbolizing the time of the Heart and the Mind coming together to work in unity. Pachakuti would come and the return of the ninth Inka, Pachakutec, would light the way to a new era. Pachakutec was seen as a man-god, the bringer of light and builder of the Inka Empire. Inka is also translated as "Light" or "Wholeness". The veils between the worlds would part and the opportunity to usher in a new world and new kind of human would not only be possible, but probable. In the Quechua language pacha means earth, time or cycle, a complete unit. There are shorter and longer pachas, cycles of time, enfolded within one another. The grand pacha or era, of approximately 26,000 years that is coming to completion marks the time of renewal, purification and the beginning of a new cycle. The indigenous visionaries and elders foresaw this as an unprecedented time of ascension of collective consciousness and awakening on a global scale. A time to reset and realign our spiritual values. Pacha also means a complete unit. We are all pachas as individuals, our heart is a pacha in and of itself and the entire galaxy is a pacha. Cycles within cycles. Pachas within pachas. Kuti means return, to turn upside down or to set things right. Pachakuti speaks of the time that we are in and the initiation we are undergoing. When we consider that humans are part of nature and the Earth, not separate from nature, we too are getting our inner worlds turned upside down and right side up. We too are being guided by the Golden Staff of Pachakuteq to awaken to the Light and Wholeness within.

It is now, in our present day that the Great Irrigation of Cosmic Light is flooding the Earth and the inner rivers of mankind. This time of higher frequencies hitting the Earth carries with it the potential of a new world being born and new kind of human being born. The Maya call this new kind of human "those that are made of honey." The new era to follow Pachakuti, the overturning of earth and time, is referred to as the Taripay Pacha or the Golden Age of "meeting ourselves again." It denotes a time of living in conscious union with our Divine nature, and living in harmony with Mother Nature, each other and all life. A beautiful possibility to bring our focused awareness to, and to consciously participate in the manifestation of this new era.

According to prophecies from around the world we have entered this stage of purification, which will lead to heightened chaos, more volatility in the environment, an exposure of false education, and an exposure of the lies and the truths that have been hidden from us by our governments. This period is said to last until around the year 2030, when the present age, the purification and how we perceive ourselves and the world around us will come to a close and the Golden Age will be fully underway. The time of the Condor and Eagle coming together, and flying wing to wing. Through their ceremonies and reverent approach to life, Indigenous people have been maintaining the tapestry, the very fabric of life, since the beginning of time. There is a call for indigenous people from all four corners of the earth, and those walking a path of beauty, to come together to share knowledge and work together to assist humanity through these chaotic times. Many of us are aware of similar prophecies. If you are not, simply look around. We don't need the prophecy of the ancients to see that our earth is suffering. The rivers and oceans are polluted. The skies are grey with pollution. War pervades so much of our land and communities. Humanity as a whole is suffering physically and spiritually. Some make money, own big houses and fancy cars, yet are unhappy. Most are living in cities with overly busy schedules and spend little or no time in nature. Bodies are stressed, immune systems are weak and no longer respond to western medicines the way they used to. We have exhausted our antibiotic arsenals and each year we have to develop a new one to combat the common cold. Our bodies no longer know how to heal themselves.

The fulfillment of our ascension and alignment with the

frequencies of the Golden Age is dependent on returning to the wisdom of the ancients. We must look back on the future to know where we are headed and to choose a more life affirming path. Will we continue to make the same mistakes or will be learn from them and choose something different?

Indigenous world views from around the globe are strikingly similar in their vision of these times. They also give unique gifts of insight for the navigation of these times. The Hopi refer to the current day as one of great purification, the end of the 4th World with the beginning of the 5th World, when the earth will return to balance and her children will once again honor the ways of nature and the feminine. The Aztec refer to this time as great transformation and the creation of a new race. The ancient calendar of the Cherokee ends at the exact time as the Mayan calendar, and the Maori predict that as the veils between the worlds dissolve, the physical world and spiritual world will merge. Parallel to the Inca prophecy, the Hindu tradition speaks of a new kind of man and a mass of enlightened ones leading the way to bright future.

The Q'ero Nation, along with other indigenous people are sharing their timeless wisdom and are revealing ancient secrets, mystical and alchemical processes that have been protected for hundreds if not thousands of years, kept hidden from the hands and minds of the masses. Why are they coming forth? Because it is time! There are now enough people on the planet who understand, who honor life and will use these teachings for a higher good, rather than for personal gain, greed, power or to control life. It is time for us to once again become proper stewards of the Earth and the destiny of humanity. We cannot continue to live on the Earth in the manner that we have and are. We are being asked to drop our fear, to illuminate our hearts and come together in unity. We are being asked to truly look at ourselves, to take responsibility for the world we have created and to set aside our personal, ego driven goals in order to be in service to the whole of humanity and the Natural World. It is time to remember the Earth as our great Mother and once again honor the feminine way. It is a beautiful time to be alive. We all need to be asking ourselves these questions every day. Do I create with loving, kind thoughts, with respect for all life and all beings? Have I cleared from my heart the lower tendencies of jealousy and envy? Have I forgiven those that have hurt me, or am I carrying anger and resentment towards them? Do I judge myself and others so harshly that it closes my heart or creates more separation? What are the filters and beliefs that I view myself, others and the world through? Does fear run my life or does courage, compassion and love run my life?

It is time to awaken to a higher calling and to work towards creating a Heaven on Earth. This is not simply a new age concept. It is something many people all over the globe are feeling, speaking about and aligning with. It is the energy of the 5th Sun and as Children of the Earth and as stewards of consciousness, it is our responsibility to fulfill it. It is each individual's responsibility to bring the New Era to life though taking responsibility for what we have created and what we continue to create with our every thought, our every word and our every action, in every moment of everyday. We have been given the great gift of physical life on this beautiful planet and it is time to give back to life. It is time to reanimate the forests and the rivers. It is time to protect the rainforest, and it is time to live with joyful service to all life. One of my mentors in South America continually refers to our life's work as our unconditional love service to the Divine Plan for the Mother Earth and Humanity. He lovingly imparted a simple yet profound prayer to start my day with. "Divine Creator, show me how I can be of service, in every moment of my life to the unfolding of the Divine Plan for the Mother Earth and all my relations." This prayer has become a daily mantra that keeps my life focused and the fire of inspiration burning.

Indigenous people view the Earth as a living being, our

Mother, who contains the fertile soil of spirit manifest in matter. Our Mother who grows all that we need to feed our bodies, nourish our spirit, heal our souls and to experience the true nature of our spirit in human form. Shamans recognize the Earth as a Living Library and the indigenous tribes around the world as the stewards and guardians of this living library that hold instructions for our return home.

Our future is not fixed, it is fluid, and what will come is based on the choices that each individual makes each moment of every day. Anything we can imagine exists within the invisible field of all possibility, no matter how far-fetched or impossible it may seem. When someone, or even better, a group of individuals imagines something, and then focuses attention on that idea or possibility, that possibility becomes a probability. When the old is crumbling before us and nothing seems to be working, we become willing to try new ways. I often hear people in a health crisis or spiritual crisis say, "I'll try or do anything at this point. I just want to get better." That is a powerful statement. We must use the opportunity at hand to expand our perceptions of self and the Universe by leaping into Unknown, into the Great Mystery.

Amidst the chaos we are living in, we are being asked to not succumb to more fear, violence or separation, but instead join hands and become stronger than ever. It's during times of pronounced challenge and crisis that one is drawn to prayer and learns to pray with more intent and heart centered energy behind the prayer. Shifting our perspective is the first step of the shaman's way to changing reality and to dreaming a different dream. Will you answer the call? Will you become a Luminous Warrior and Way Shower?

We are living in a time of fulfillment of the prophecy. In a time of unprecedented change and unparalleled opportunity in the history of mankind, and whether we realize it or not, we each hold a key to the unfolding and the birth of this new era.

Each and everyone one of us is responsible for and have the gift of discovering our authentic nature and our soul's purpose with more support than ever before available. We are all being called to heal the wounds of our individual and collective past, to dismantle our egotism, limiting beliefs and judgments that we place on ourselves and others. It is a time to be grateful, a time to learn humility and a time to simplify our lives. It is a time to be brave and courageous.

And so, I chose to further awaken to my role as a Guardian of the Earth and a bridge of the ancient wisdom. I have also chosen to answer the call of writing this book, with the intention of creating, in full participation with the frequencies of the 5th Sun and Golden Age of the Taripay Pacha. It has been a long, windy, bumpy, yet ultimately empowering experience.

Mount Munay and the 7 Saiwas

Now, let's dive in to the magic of the Andean tradition and the 7 Saiwas.

In an ancient Andean myth, Wiracocha, (Creator), knowing that man would forget their origins, constructed and raised an ethereal staircase of Universal Law on the horizon of Mount Munay (moon - eye). The Ladder of Cosmic Light was to assist mankind in re-establishing their inner connection to the Divine and to reach higher levels of consciousness during their time on Earth. The 7 Saiwas (sigh - wahs), Universal Laws, created the cosmic staircase of light that connects the Heavens and Earth, the celestial with physical, Spirit with Human. Wiracocha built this etheric staircase to provide a map and bridge to awakening, a path to living in Ayni (eye-knee), and a bridge to transforming consciousness. The Andean people believe that each child is born into the world perfectly aligned with these 7 Saiwas, born from Divine Consciousness. As the child grows and becomes conditioned and programmed with the beliefs and values most prevalent in their environment and society, their alignment to the 7 Saiwas becomes diffused. The journey of the Andean Paqo (Shaman) is to climb to the summit of Mount Munay, (unconditional love), and take his/her place on the peak.

Through the embodiment and living in ayni with the 7 Saiwas, the transformation of consciousness into Divine consciousness, and the remembering of our purest, un-corrupted Self is attainable. Each step of the sacred staircase represents one of the 7 Saiwas, which are organic Universal Laws providing a map of orientation, and guide the initiate on their journey through the Kaypacha, the physical reality, in which we have the opportunity to attain enlightenment in physical form.

Cosmo-vision is the world view of a society that is deeply embedded in the way in which that society is organized and evolves over time. It is a society's way of explaining and better understanding all that surrounds it. Indigenous societies such as the Andean culture are organized around high ceremonial centers, and sacred sites which were constructed to reflect the cosmos through architecture and placement in direct relation to celestial bodies. These centers are places where divine power reaches the earth and is channeled. These centers held ritual events that gave the people access to making or generating that which aligns with their Cosmo-vision.

Living in sacred reciprocity, in a continual state of energetic exchange with the living world of energy and Spirit that animates all life, is the essence and meaning of Ayni. It is to bring harmony to our inner and outer world, to create meaning with spiritually aligned, sacred interactions with all life. We will go deeper into the meaning of Ayni throughout this book. Saiwa refers to a stone obelisk that is used as a marker. An obelisk is defined as a pillar of stone, especially one built as a monument, that has a square base and sides that taper like a pyramid toward a pointed top. A more spiritual and mystical description of saiwa is that of a shaft of light or pillar or light. This shaft of Light is what unites the three worlds, the Hanaq pacha (upper world or celestial realms), the Kay pacha (the physical realm our bodies inhabit), and the Ukhu pacha (the lower world or domain of the unconscious). It is the etheric shaft of light that unites our High Self, our Conscious Self and our Lower Self.

Although the myth describes these saiwas as a cosmic staircase, the path to Heaven and the peak of Mount Munay, it is not linear. Therefore, each of the saiwas is not be seen as a path in which you first master this saiwa and then the next one. The image of a lotus flower is a more accurate depiction of how this body of Universal Law and spiritual principles dwell and enfold within one another.

An Andean paqo understands that it is her degree of integrity that enables her to integrate and bring these seven principles to life, determining her level of consciousness and her potential to co-create and live in harmony with the totality of creation. She understands that information is transformed into power, (conscious awareness/understanding) through this flowering map of the 7 Saiwas, becoming a *chakaruna,* the one who bridges wisdom for others, and helps others cross from one state of consciousness to another. Another way to understand this is that information grows into wisdom as experience happens consciously. She also understands that through the embodiment process, meaning is created and lived. When one is not living consciously, experiences are repeated over and over again, re-creating different versions of the same story. Thus, embodying these 7 Saiwas is a practical, efficient and spiritual practice of energy management, consciousness, mastering our lives and our spiritual nature.

"We are all part of the living energy, the web of life. We come from wholeness. This is reality. Separateness is an illusory state of mind."
Chandra Sun Eagle

Kausay

Kausay, (cow-sigh), the Living Energy, is the Quechua word for what the yogis of ancient times call prana, what the Chinese call Chi and the Hawaiians term mana. Kausay, the multi-dimensional energy of creation and animating force of the cosmos, is the essential fuel and the life-force that infuses everything in the universe, visible and invisible. It is the living energy matrix that connects all life and forms the web of life. Feeding, maintaining and harmonizing the web of life through ritual and ceremonial practices is one of The Andean Paqo's great responsibilities and gift to life. Kausay is the life-force that creates galaxies, suns, mountains, plants, animals and humans through its various expressions and vibrational frequencies. This interconnected web of energy is what the Q'ero call the Kausay Pacha or World of Living Energy. Kausay is the primal energy of creation that is in continuous flow and it is an ongoing process that encircles all existence. Nothing is absent of this life-force.

When one is in a living, breathing relationship with Kausay the emphasis and expression of life shifts into a more energetic and Spiritually focused life, opening channels of consciousness that draws one closer to becoming an awakened light being. For the Paqo, living with optimum life force is an essential to developing the fullness and the embodiment of power and full participation with creation. Increasing and becoming familiar with one's own life force, while learning to invoke and harness the forces of nature is absolutely necessary on the shamanic path as well as for anyone wishing to live with more vitality and well-being. The primary and absolute necessity for deepening our place in creation and our connection to source energy is through the identification with ourselves beyond a physical form that is solitary. An identification with the stars, the mountains, the rivers, and the power places of earth, the plants, trees and animals lift us into more expanded knowing and experiencing of who we truly are and where we come from. The Andean people live with the knowing that they are Children of the Sun. and Children of the Earth. The powers found in the earth and in the cosmos are communed with and honored as a part of their everyday life. Prayerful offerings are made daily in order to tend to the balance of the human sphere, the forces of nature and the elements.

Kausay is the gift of life. It is food for the Soul, food for our subtler energy bodies and thus it is food for our physical body. We receive Kausay from nature, the air we breathe, known as Kausay wayra (why-ra), energy from light of the sun and light of the celestial realms, known as Kausay kanchay (kaun-chai), and we receive Kausay directly from the Earth herself, known as Kausay pacha. When the flow of kausay is impeded, there is a lack of life force to flow through us. Impeded life force can be due to poor air quality, not enough time in nature, EMF frequencies from cell phones, computers, televisions, or eating too much processed food and not enough live foods. An imbalance between work and play, too much stress and our life force becomes weak, our immune systems become compromised and disease can manifest. Our life force can also be compromised by prolonged states of worry, unhealthy emotions, such as jealousy, anger, resentment or fear. Everything we eat, think, feel and do has an effect on our energy level and how well the elixir of life is flowing through and informing us.

Re-establishing a connection to the living energy through re-gaining membership to the land, to the pacha mama and to the celestial realms will return you to your rightful place within the order of creation. Infinite amounts of energy are available to all.

Learning to harness, command and "push" Kausay, is an

act of power for the Paqo, not in the way of having control or power over, but in working with living energy to bring flow and nurturance to all life. The power to create and the power to manifest more of what we need and want in our lives. We have to have power to create. When referring to power, I am talking about the purity of potential to manifest or to make something happen, when one's intentions, thoughts and actions are aligned with Spirit and the Highest Good. We need life force to get things done. We need it to have good health and we need to be able to compost and transmute, or mikhuy (mee - qui), the heavy energies that accumulate in our lives and in our environments. The more Kausay we have flowing through us, the more our energy body stays full and we are able to generate energy in our daily life, rather than depleting it. If we do get depleted, we can recharge and refill our tank with less effort. The word power in the western world has become filled with connotations of something bad or egoic. Which yes, we all know that it is a person's choice and morals that direct how that power will be used. Pure potential/power is just power. That is until the one wielding the power decides the manner in which it will be applied and for what purposes.

The relationship of The Living Energy and Ayni

To understand ayni is to understand the essence of the Andean culture and the foundation of their daily, spiritually based lives. Ayni, for the native peoples of the Andes, is the foundation from which their lives are based. Ayni is an organizing principle of sacred reciprocity that leads to right relationship and governs their daily existence, work ethics and spiritual codices. The nature of ayni, which is a balanced exchange of giving and receiving, exists in the energy world and is the reality of a higher order within the fabric of physical life. Cultivating ayni cannot be accomplished to its greatest expression without being in a conscious and participatory relationship with the world of the living energy. Honoring and having reverence for all life, while creating congruent and harmonious relationships; harmonious relationship with ourselves, our families and communities, a harmonious relationship with the Mother Earth, the animals, the plants, the elements and a harmonious relationship with Creator is to be in ayni. If or when you go to the Andes of Peru you will be enveloped instantly and experience ayni in its fullest expression. The people are warm and open, and their generous spirits can be felt immediately. Farmers are making offerings of flowers and wine to the Mother Earth and to the land spirits before harvesting. They feed the Pacha Mama with chocolates, sweets and grains, symbolizing their gratitude for all the abundance she has and will grow for them, before planting their seeds. Recognizing the Earth Mother as a living breathing being who cares for them on a physical and spiritual level, Pacha Mama provides the sustenance with which they feed their bodies and their animals and the trees and clay from which they make their homes. The Mother Earth is revered as the physical manifestation of the all-pervasive Cosmic Mother.

Ayni is created through a continual cultivation and exchange of unconditional giving and receiving. To live and create from a place of ayni, with a conscious mindset and recognition that we are part of a larger organism, and that we are intrinsically connected to all life on an energetic level, is the key to realizing and experiencing our Oneness with all life. Reverence and respect for all life, including ourselves, is essential. Every moment of life, we are in a continual interplay of energy exchange. Becoming conscious and intentional with the exchanges we are having and creating in our lives allows us to evaluate the areas of life in which we are in ayni and those areas that we are not. When our lives are governed by reverence and sacred reciprocity, our lives and the lives around us tend to flourish and flow with more grace. Synchronicity becomes more of the norm rather than the occasional event. We meet the right person at the right time, or the next book we need to read jumps off the shelf at the bookstore. We hear the same message from a song or people we meet on the street in the course of few days, bringing clarity to a decision we need to make, or pointing us in the right direction of life.

Being in ayni with ourselves is also about being in touch with our personal gifts, talents and innate wisdom, and bringing these gifts into the world. Many hold themselves back from sharing their talents, personal gifts or self-expression due to fear and other reasons. When we do this, we are blocking the flow of sacred exchange within and without and the flow of Kausay is blocked. We are each a spoke on the great wheel of life. Our beauty and soul expression are a very important part of the whole and needed to bring the human family and all our relations together.

Over the years I have come to understand the profundity of ayni and the many layers and areas that this organizing principle needs to be reestablished and woven back into the consciousness and lives of those existing in the western world. Many in the western culture seem to have lost their way and have forgotten the way of ayni.

Encoded within Inca Mythology are the treasures of an ancient wisdom encrypted through astronomy, the ideals and the spiritual principles of the Andean People - myths linked to the cosmos that were meant to sail the seas of time. The Andean people live in a world that has meaning and purpose and to them that meaning is created by modeling Earth and their lives after the Heavens, mirroring back the harmony of God's Creation and the cosmos in their cities, in their sacred sites, in the terracing of the mountain sides and the valley floors and creating Ayni on Earth as it is mirrored in the Heavens. The Inca left a map of their Cosmo-vision etched into the very landscape of the Sacred Urubamba Valley. The entire Milky Way and its constellations are represented in the Sacred Valley. Effigies of the condor, the serpent, the toad, the llama, the fox and other beings that either formed naturally and/or were constructed through the shapes of their stone walls, can still be seen, while many of the effigies are seen only by the eyes of the initiate. Running through the Urubamba Valley is the Urubamba River. Mirroring the Urubamba River on the Pacha Mama is the sacred river in the sky known as the Wilka Mallyu, which for the Inka is the causeway that links the land of the gods to the human physical realm, creating ayni between the celestial and earthly realms.

To be and live in ayni is to harmonize and unify the three fundamental aspects of the soul, the three levels of consciousness and the three levels of reality. These three selves are most commonly known as our High Self, the Conscious Self and the Basic or elemental self, known in the Andean Cosmology as our Condor Essence, Puma essence and our Serpent Essence.

Fundamentals of the Andean Cosmo-Vision

Many of you reading this book are familiar with the cosmology of the Andean culture and spiritual tradition. For those who are new to this, the following information will provide the basic foundation and primary principles of how they view, and therefore, how they organize and co-create with the living world of energy, a Cosmo-vision that mirrors Heaven on Earth.

The Three Worlds

In the Andean cosmology, as well as within most indigenous societies, the universe is seen to exist as three levels of reality, or on three planes of existence, through which a central column runs and connects the three worlds. This axis, also known as the world tree, has long been known to shamans of all traditions, and provides the shaman an energetic causeway to all levels of reality. This axis is referred to as a saiwa or shaft of light in Quechua. We, as humans, are light beings, Children of the Sun. We are multi-dimensional beings with aspects of our souls existing in all three realms. In the Andes, these three realms are referred to as the three worlds, the Ukhu pacha (uhu-pawcha), the Kay pacha (kie-pawcha), and the Hanaq pacha (hanak-pawcha). The three worlds are intimately connected and interwoven. Paqos and shamans must journey into and map these realms, becoming intimately familiar with the territory, for their own healing, to bring healing for others and to create ayni - integrating and mastering connection with the three worlds, creating harmony and balance between them and within us.

Kay pacha is loosely translated as middle or outer. It is the world of matter in which we live. It is the reality that most people in the western world feel is the only reality, because we can see it with our eyes and touch it with our hands. For the Paqo the Kay pacha is an animate world where the elements and the spirit world intercede. Where the invisible informs the visible and we have the opportunity to awaken to higher consciousness while in human form.

Hanaq pacha is loosely translated as upper or transcendent, and is the domain of the transcendent. It can be thought of as the realm of heaven and the stars, the realm of higher vibration, where order and illumination are prominent. It is the stars from which we come, and the stars that hold the seeds to our becoming. It is the realm of luminous beings, divine helpers, and where ascended masters reside. Our highest destiny is found when we connect with the Hanaq pacha.

The Ukhu pacha is loosely translated as under or inner. The Ukhu pacha, is known as the underworld, the belly of the Pacha Mama, and is inhabited by aspects of the individual and the collective unconscious. This domain is also pregnant with the un-potentiated energy of the Pacha Mama and the fertile and fluid qualities of the serpent, kundalini, energies of creation.

The Archetypes of the three worlds - the Trilogy

Each of the three worlds has corresponding symbology and

archetypal forces. The archetype, and organizing principle of the Kay pacha, is governed by the Choca Chinchay, the jaguar or puma. Bringing order to chaos, puma walks in balance, in grace and beauty, teaching the ways of impeccability and integrity. Puma's warrior strength invokes in the initiate the qualities of stability, and the courage to awaken the master and teacher within, while teaching us how to be comfortable in solitude and content within. Representing the life/death principle, the puma brings us deeper into relationship with the natural world and our instinctual nature. She is the one who walks by our side, showing us the way beyond death and into infinite possibility. Puma, the peaceful warrior who lives and walks in peace and synchronicity with life, without needing to be seen.

Sachamama, the serpent, is the archetype of the underworld. Sachamama, also referred to as Amaru, is the mother of the waters, the awakened one who brings healing and activation of primary life force, the kundalini. She teaches us how to heal and shed past wounds, while flowing with the rhythms of life. She awakens in the initiate the mastery of change and transition, while reconnecting us to the fluid body and fluid nature of creation. She is the one who knows the way back to the garden, back to innocence: guiding us to the deepest places of wellbeing and fertility.

Apuchin, the great condor is the archetype and organizing principle of the Hanaq pacha. The condor is the messenger from the cosmos and connects us to our high self, the seer and visionary. Reminding us how to soar with our winged, celestial nature and yet connected with the Earthly plane, through expanded vision of the heart and becoming a messenger of the heavens. The condor is a symbol of luminosity and soaring into the freedom of Luminous Awareness and Light.

We each have a Condor/Eagle essence, a Puma essence and a Serpent essence, which when recovered and embodied, activate our natural instincts, and assist us in understanding how the three worlds and the three fundamental levels of consciousness live within us.

Becoming a powerful conductor of kausay
The Luminous Energy Field

It is not my intention to go into the depths of the Luminous energy field, as it is well documented in several books, which I highly recommend, written by Alberto Villoldo, Ph.D. I do feel it is important to touch on it briefly to give you more understanding of how the Andean medicine people view and approach ayni and work with the living energy. In essence, from the shamanic perspective, our relative truths, stories, wounds and events of the past, reside on an energetic level as imprints that are embedded in the blue print of our Luminous Energy Field (LEF). Our luminous energy field is our personal energy bubble that envelops the body, and connects to us physically through the chakra system. Imprints, which create affinities, inform and organize our external reality as well as our physical and internal realities. Like attracts like. Every experience we have ever endured is etched into the LEF creating a blueprint, predisposing us to repeating the same conditions over and over. Through shamanic practices known to indigenous people around the world, such as soul retrieval, imprint clearing, chakra illumination, ritual and ceremonial alignment with the three worlds, the shaman is able clear old affinities and rewire one's luminous architecture to the essential, (Kollana), to the Absolute, (Munay), and reestablish balance between people and the environment. Becoming aware and in tune with your luminous energy field puts you in touch with a great gift of self-empowerment. Knowing what is imprinted in our LEF, affords us the ability to heal and dissolve what is not creating beauty in our life, and the ability to rewire our LEF with timeless, essential forces of creation. When we are wired with kausay and living in Ayni we become a vessel through which great action happens with less effort. Life becomes easier, less of a struggle and more fulfilling.

Munay, Yachay and Llankay

Andean Shamans do recognize the 7 major chakras, as well as smaller ones in the energy body, which are located in the palms, the bottoms of the feet. The main difference for them is that the 2nd (llankay), the 4th (munay), and the 6th (yachay), are the primary energy centers when it comes to organizing energies of the three worlds and three levels of consciousness. Each of these three centers has its own vibration, wave length and quality, and is connected to particular domains within the Upper World, Middle World and Lower World. The chakras located above and below three primary centers of exchange act as secondary energy centers.

The inner realm of the Kay pacha is situated in our heart chakra. The Quechua word for center and heart is Sonqo/sonco. It is within this energetic center, the place between the lower three chakras and the upper three chakras that all energies converge and from which all things emerge. The center. It is the work of the initiate to awaken the heart of Munay, the absolute truth, the compassionate, timeless and impersonal love of the creator that weaves together all life. It is the fabric of existence. Munay is beyond personal or romantic love and it is the initiate's responsibility to cultivate this "way of being" and to do their service from this place of perception/awareness.

The inner realm of the Hanaq pacha is situated within the 6th chakra of the energy body. The place of thought and vision, referred to as yachay (ya-chai). When the Hanaq pacha is awakened within the individual, the third eye is opened and thought is transformed from random, continuous chatter, to the peaceful, empty, and cosmic wisdom of the "infinite mind". For the Andean shaman, awakening to this level is not achieved through meditation, prayer and visualization alone. It is also necessary to bring personal knowledge, gained through study, ceremony, and life experience, into Oneness with the transcendent, through consciously embodying, and living in congruence with munay, the state of unconditional love.

The inner realm of the Ukhu pacha is situated in the energy center known as the 2nd chakra, and is referred to as llankay (yawn-kie), the center through which we connect with our deepest passions and then bring that passion into alignment with our service the world. Llankay is the principle of yachay (thought), and munay, (the absolute), in action through our service and work in the world. Ultimately it is when we have unified the will of the heart with knowledge and proper thinking that our actions become a spontaneous and instinctual act of heart and mind harmonization.

The system of connectivity

Ceke systems are fundamental to creation in the Andean tradition. Cekes are the vibration and/or energy binder that bring together parts of a structure that have commonalities. It is through the sensitivity to and the use of the ceke system that the shaman is able to weave the cosmos, the forces of nature and inner earth realms into her mesa and into her luminous architecture.

You may also know cekes and ceke systems as the ley lines that run through the earth, connecting sacred sites, energetic vortices and places of power. It is from the energetic center of Cusco, known as the Coricancha, that cekes run horizontally, hundreds of miles in all directions to form the Inka empire, or Taywantinsuyu, and connect all the sacred altars. From all the sacred altars, cekes run vertically to the celestial realms, connecting the stars and constellations to the earth altars and the Apus.

Cekes are also the cords in the energy body that bind us to other times, people and places. We are all bound by different aspects of personal and collective karma and the energy cords that hold karma in place on the Earth. As we do our own healing and awakening work, we are also healing and loosening the karmic holds of our ancestors and on the planet.

In the language of energy there are three types of cekes, kayao, payan and kollana.

Kayao is considered tertiary or literal. This type of ceke is a consequence of time and space, particularly of this time and space that tend to form the majority of our collective story, ceke systems, people's personal beliefs and myths, and the consensual reality of the western world.

Payan is considered the secondary expression of source energy into form and also has to do with time and space, but not necessarily this time and space. An example of this would be karmic threads to memories and/or identification with past life experiences.

Kollana is the energy of the essential and the timeless. It is not bound by time or space and is the same energy that could be found 200 or 20,000 years ago. For the paqo it is essential to establish a clear relationship to kollana, as it is primary energy that brings one into communion with their eternal nature and wholeness, and has the ability to transform instantly. With well-established cekes the paqo is able to call in and source from places of power thousands of miles away and bring that energy into her body and the space or person she is helping.

Within these three types of cekes there is an infinite number of ways they manifest and become filters through which we see and perceive the world. Cekes have a fluid structure and can vary in their complexity, making them less or more potent in their effect on the person(s) or situation. I use the word potent in reference to the magnitude of the energetic connection. For the paqo to become a masterful healer and weaver of creation, it is crucial to know the nature of her cekes, and to clear or shift payan and kayao relationships into qualities of kollana, timeless, primordial and eternal energy, adopting kollana as her primary source of existence.

During a healing it is vital for the paqo to be able to track and find the source of a client's issue in relation to the nature of the ceke. This is necessary for determining what type of healing is needed and for the healing to be of lasting effect, otherwise the pattern or symptoms will most likely return. A shamanic healer is a facilitator, mediator and harmonizer, who has access to a lot of energy and a lot of Light. She knows how to wield the energy and guide the person towards self-empowerment.

Assemblage Point

On the edge of the bubble or cocoon of energy that surrounds us, the LEF, we all have what is called the assemblage point. The assemblage point is a combination of all the bundles of perception, social and ancestral imprints that create specific vibrations of resonance, and then attract and invite in that which is in resonance with it. Information and energy always find the resonance receptors it has affinities with.

The Paqo develops, within the framework of their Life, a means of awareness to connect actively with the sources of life, and wire these forces into their Luminous Energy Body, their Medicine Body. This way, no matter what is going on or what personal transformation is under way, they can move out of the personal and into a clear state of awareness and connection with Universal forces. They then can do their work, perform ceremonies and healing without their personal process getting in the way. In the western world, due in large to perceiving mostly through the mind and duality, the majority of people's assemblage points can be found in the head area, and information is filtered through their personal prejudices and beliefs. The work of the shaman is to clear and refine these filters of the conceptual, literal and temporal realms, and reorient their awareness to the primordial living energy, while moving and maintaining their assemblage point to the Heart, in alignment with the axis. This is an ever-evolving process of creation and recreation. We move the assemblage point by cultivating luminous awareness, opening our dialogue with Heaven and Earth, and wiring cekes of light from the three worlds, or domains, the land and power places into our energy bubble. We are then able to exercise existence in a totally different way. We have more latitude in life, are able to call in and work with our spiritual lineage and big forces of energy. Our entire life and energy field becomes an assemblage point for the new era and we are able to accelerate evolution, quantum leap into a new timeline and craft reality from a higher, more expansive vantage point. The timeline I speak of is Creator's timeline, and it is what we answer to. We also do this sacred work, exercise and express the exchange of energetic forces through ceremony and the body of Mesa.

The Paqo's Mesa

The mesa is the Paqo's altar and is a living embodiment of the macrocosm, and a repository of frequencies that they draw upon to awaken deep states of individual and collective healing. It is an animistic tapestry of sacred items and symbolic power objects that are infused with Kollana Kausay (essential energy), harnessed from the forces of nature, power places, Mother Earth and Spirit Energy. A resource of energy and connectedness, based on their personal gifts, skill set, and hapu rantis, the mesa is a reflection of the Paqo's life force and the various types of Kausay they have learned to wield. Hapu means power or great, and ranti means relationship. Finding and nurturing the hapu rantis becomes a primary focus for the Paqo, and then weaving these forces of power into their mesa and into their energy field through shamanic energy practices that establish a living ceke system within their luminous energy field. Once the luminous energy field is wired with hapu rantis the shaman is then able channel and mediate universal and earthly energies into the space. The energies and forces available to them are not determined solely by personal energy alone, but by greater forces, hence the potential for transformation is exponential and instantaneous healing and miracles happen. On the path of the Alto Mesalloq (Mountain shaman), the body becomes the mesa. Together, through their medicine body and the tapestry of the mesa, the Paqo becomes a magnetic receptacle for Universal forces. Energy is gathered, organized and then transmitted to the living body of the Earth for planetary healing, or to the body of a person for healing.

Each Paqo's mesa is connected with the mesa of his or her elders, their lineage, main sponsor mountain and with all the ancient mesa carriers through the ceremonial altars and places of power, known as Huacas (Waw-kas), where the energies of heaven and earth meet. Huacas are portals or doorways to other realms and are repositories for tremendous amounts of Kausay. Through each Paqo's connection to Higher Light, Creator Light, a web of Light forms and creates pathways to each altar and each Paqo. Light multiples Light! Each time a paqo, shaman or healer of the lineage asks for or lends assistance through this Light network of huacas, the Light grows and the energy amplifies, which is another way the organizing principle of cooperation expresses itself in the Andes. There is no need for competition of who is a more powerful Paqo, as every Paqo is recognized as integral part of the whole, with their own specialties and gifts that never detract from Light, but only amplify it.

Huacas were built or had formed naturally in the shaped of an animal or bird that represented a constellation within the southern sky. The Andean people believe they come from the stars and when they die, they return to their homeland huaca within the stars. Each tribe and its homeland huaca, despite their different star origins, different languages and customs, are all united as children of the common Creator and of the Stars, each tribe representing a constellation in the sky. So, in the same way that the stars have their unique qualities and distinct location in the Milky Way, but move together in harmony, the Andean People live and work under the same principle and ideals, that of Ayni - Sacred Reciprocity and Right Relationship through cooperation. The celestial realms reflect order, and such is the way of the Andean life, to live in unison with each other and the Earth, mirroring back to the heavens and Creator, organizing every aspect of their lives with Divine Cosmic Order in the Sky. They employ the timing and cycles of the stars to govern their planting and harvesting seasons. Living in communion with the Celestial Realms while anchoring Spirit into the physical plane is to live in Ayni.

Refining the architecture of your LEF and life requires diligence, self-inquiry, non-attachment, acceptance, an abundance of trust, the willingness to be vulnerable, and the ability to be completely honest with one's self. It also takes an enormous amount of courage. I can remember being very scared to let go of certain cords or cekes. It often meant I would be letting go of a familiar point of reference, would be risking losing a relationship or would be detaching even more from what was considered normal and accepted by society. The conscious restructuring of agreements I had with myself and others proved to be a challenge in accepting the invitation to step up in consciousness and in my service. The beauty and expansion experienced through the letting go, and the shifting of my internal awareness, was that gradually the true nature of reality began to reveal itself to me. The process of letting go, or cutting certain cords can also be frightening because it can feel like a part of you or your life has died, which in a way it has. But for the Paqo, a meaningful and fulfilled life is one of many deaths and many births, a continuous dance with creation, shifting from form to formless and back into form with the ultimate and absolute truth being "eternal love."

Morphogenic Fields

On a recent wintery, late afternoon, as I hiked in the final moments of the day's light, enjoying the fresh mountain air and the beauty around me, I consciously gathered Kausay with each breath and each step. My mind was quiet and focused on my practice. Just before reaching the top a window in the clouds formed, giving way to thick streams of golden sun light. The magnificence of the energy pouring through was overwhelmingly beautiful and I was feeling lighter and lighter with each step. I reached the top and my body came to a relaxed stance. I could feel the bubble of my energy body expanding as the ingress of light into my chakras created an increase in their vitality and bandwidth, and then an outward movement from my three primary centers. The ingress and outward movement went on for only a couple of minutes until I could no longer distinguish me from the sun. It was then that I heard, "We are always influencing the morphogenic field through our light body and chakra system." I was experiencing the download energetically. It was being shown to me through the interchange of my Light Body. Being familiar with the process taking place, and knowing that I could risk cluttering the airwaves with my own thoughts or reaching to understand, I stood in quiet until I felt my field begin to contract slowly back in as the transmission completed. I left a gratitude infused pinch of tobacco as an offering and walked back home in silence, listening for more information and letting the transmission soak in deeply. Knowing there was more information to this download, I decided to dream on it before doing any research. From early on in my shamanic training I was encouraged to always seek the answers within first and through direct experience. In the morning, I remembered pieces of information from the night and then continued the inquiry in a meditative state before checking to see if what I was receiving and understanding was accurate. I was quite happy to find that what came through was in accordance with my research. The following, I was told, was to be added to the chapter on Kausay.

Morphogenic fields are invisible fields of energy that contain the blueprint or templates of conscious light and sound, that then define and instruct the development of the structure of the entire biology of all living beings. These light and sound encoded templates also determine how consciousness will manifest. Akin to the intelligence of the architect, morphogenic fields are the intelligence that guide and organize the development of all form from a microcosmic level to a macrocosmic level.

Morphogenic fields are made of parts, which are in turn, parts of the whole that are organized by energy, and become the functional organizing force of all living organisms. All organic matter, plant, animal, and human forms have manifested from the encoded imprints held within the morphogenic and morphogenetic fields.

Each of us have a personal morphogenetic field, referred to as the Luminous Energy Field in the Andes, that is connected and exchanges information and energy with other planetary, galactic and universal fields. This is called morphogenic resonance. Depending on what and how our Luminous Energy Field is imprinted and wired determines what we are in resonance with, what we attract into our life and therefore, what is reinforced or recreated on a personal level as well as a collective level. The exact definition of morphogenic resonance is the act of similar forms reverberating and exchanging information within a Universal Life Force.

The chakras are the vital applications running the circuitry of the energy body and physical body that move these fields of morphogenic energy through our being. The chakras organize, develop and maintain our physical, mental and spiritual health and wellbeing.

In Rupert Sheldrake's research he found that there is a

continuous spectrum of morphic fields, including morphogenetic fields, behavior fields, mental fields and social and societal fields. If we expand our view and consider that each of us are multidimensional beings that have had several past lives, we can see that there are levels within levels and fields within fields of blueprints that are all interconnected.

Through my own healing and assisting others, I've come to understand that the programs embedded in the subconscious and in the chakra system are either in morphic resonance with healthy, higher vibrational fields, or lower vibrational fields that are less empowering or totally disempowering.

Let's take a quick walk through the chakras, the possible programming, and the subsequent fields that these programs and beliefs create affinities with, and bind our energy to. The chakras are like portals, assemblage points and access points to the inner planes and the spiritual realms. This is a brief summary but should give some good context to what we are speaking about in relation to our energy bodies and levels of consciousness as they interrelate with the Quantum Field, and the sub fields found within it. When we bring energy in from one of these fields, we bring it in through one of or a number of our chakras at any given moment.

1st Chakra

Referred to as the root chakra, the first chakra is located at the base of the spine and connects us energetically to the Mother Earth. Outdated ancestral programming around lack, scarcity, and fear of survival tend to affect the root chakra dramatically and can lead to feeling unsafe in the world, ungrounded, not trusting the body, not having enough of what need to survive physically, and not being able to care of oneself. Not being able to create healthy boundaries for oneself is another sign that the root chakra is running these types of programs. When we have healthy programs anchored in the 1st chakra and connected with coherent morphogenic fields we feel grounded, safe, a sense of self identity and belonging and we are able manifest our needs and desires on a physical level supported.

2nd Chakra

The second or sacral chakra is located just below the belly button. This energy center is the seat of our creativity, our sexuality and primal emotions. It is governed by the element of water. It's strongly linked with our self-expression, our comfort level with intimacy and the ability to relax into the flow of creation, and giving us feeling of being able to fully let our creativity blossom and the ease to nurture it, connecting us to fields of hope. If we have distorted programming or imprints around sexuality, if we are holding guilt or resentment, victim consciousness or don't feel safe to open up emotionally with others, the sacral chakra will most likely be energetically wired to fields of depression, and/or addiction. We might feel helpless, constrained or hopeless.

3rd Chakra

Located just below the sternum, the third chakra is also called the solar plexus and is governed by the fire element. With a healthy third chakra one feels authentically confident and in charge of oneself. There is strong sense of self-worth, vitality, productivity and the ability to take action in one's life. It's here in the third chakra that issues to do with cutting others down, aggression and having to dominant others in order to feel powerful or get attention will show up. A lack of self-confidence and feeling of "what's the point. Nothing really matters. Who I am and what I do doesn't matter," are all indicators that work is needed to heal issues of having been dominated over, controlled, over criticized or ignored as child, to reestablish a healthy and strong sense of worth and self-confidence. so that life can become easier and less of a struggle.

4th Chakra

A flourishing, open and healthy chakra expresses as an openness to give and receive love, to have compassion and kindness towards self and others, along with feelings of inspiration and joy, which become magnetic and draw more of this type of energy into our lives. When the heart is scarred from feeling rejected, betrayed or disappointed from dreams not coming to fruition, energetic walls will build wanting to protect the heart. The chakra will then resonate and connect us to fields of resentment, feeling lackluster for life, or a lack of excitement. The flow of passion for life shuts down, and a coldness or bitterness towards life can easily take hold. Is there passion burning in your heart? Do you allow love in? Are you a person of generous spirit or have you restricted the flow of love due to fear of being hurt, rejected or betrayed? Have you forgiven others for the hurts you feel they caused you? Have you asked for forgiveness? And have you forgiven yourself?

5th Chakra

Considered the seat of our self-expression and communication, this energy center is located in the throat region and governs not only our speech, but also our ability to listen to others without judgement, and to share verbally who we are. Those with a balanced and developed 5th chakra are able to hear the subliminal, that which the other may want to express but is not. The third step of manifestation happens through this energy center. What are you speaking into existence through the words you choose and stories you tell? A healthy throat chakra shows up as the ease to speak one's truth, comfort in sharing how one feels and an ability to speak kindly and positively. The addiction to gossip, verbally attacking others, or habitual patterns of talking too much and never truly listening to others, are all indicators that a person does not actually feel secure in themselves. Deep wounding around not being heard and not given enough attention, or the opposite of always being made the center of attention, will create imbalances in the throat chakra, linking this center to lower vibrational fields such as self-aggrandizement, narcissistic tendencies, lying to either get attention or cover an insecurity, and not listening to others when it doesn't interest you. What were the messages sent to you as a child? Were you given the attention you needed? Were you heard or did you have to scream or have a tantrum to get noticed? The words and stories we speak, the cadence and tonality of our voice all carry and transmit a tremendous amount of energy.

6th chakra

Known as the third eye or brow chakra, the 6th chakra has to do with perceptions, beliefs and the filters through which we see the world. Blocks and imbalances in the 6th chakra show up as being overly analytical, theoretically always right, being judgmental or suspicious of others motivations, leading to a hyper alertness and inability to relax. Sub-fields associated with these patterns can also lead to blocked intuition and doubt, which results in confusion. Not being able to visualize your future and repressed imagination are also side effects of an unhealthy or negatively programmed 6th chakra. Judgements create complications within yourself and with Light and connect you to things you don't want to be connected to. An expanded and balanced brow chakra is linked with fields of visionary qualities, optimism, opened mindedness, spiritual knowledge and new ideas. The mind is relaxed and you are able to enter into lucid states of awareness, where the higher centers of the mind can activate and link with the universal mind. Deep focus, clarity, and insights for your next steps in life are inspired by the visionary within when this center is open and connected to higher, more stable fields. The power of non-resistant thought allows for freshness, joy and inspiration to come in.

7th Chakra

Our connectedness to pure consciousness, Universal intelligence and to Spirit come through an open and stable crown chakra. There is a connection and profound feeling of being connected Source. An understanding of cosmic law beyond cognition, language and words creates a strong sense of sovereignty, expansiveness and trust in Divine timing. Letting someone else dictate your spiritual knowledge, handing your power over or submitting to a guru or religious dogma, will often distort or close this energy center and result in feeling cut off from your own power, your own knowing and your high self.

We are constantly influencing the collective morphogenic fields through what we are thinking, how we are feeling and acting. When thinking and feeling in accordance with a particular field of information we are reinforcing that field or template, exchanging energy and reverberating with that field through morphic resonance. On the other hand, when we break free of an old pattern, an outdated ancestral programming or collective memory, a trauma and the karmic fields those patterns are entangled in, the old morphogenic fields associated begin to lose energy and as a result begin to dissolve. When the wounds are healed, forgiveness is practiced, the energy is redirected, the old beliefs let go, there is no more energy to sustain that old template and it eventually dissipates. It is like washing or cleaning the energy field of hardened, crystallized energy that has locked a certain set of patterns and prevailing beliefs in place. The field can then be re-vibrated and restored to its original Divine Blueprint.

Conversely, when an individual or group of individuals awakens to a new idea, and shifts their thinking and behaviors in order to operate within the parameters of the new idea, a new paradigm is set in motion and a New Morphogenetic Field is created. A new template is formed. Each time a person performs an act that is in resonance with this new template that new template and morphogenic field is reinforced. This is the process we are in now. The Pacha Kuti. The purification and dissolving of a past paradigm before a new one can be created and brought to life.

Recognizing the immaterial presence of intelligence as the primary developmental factor of all life is fundamental to understanding life, how it takes shape, the universe and everything in it. And as conscious co-creators we have the potential to shift our world paradigm. It is also very possible to change our biology and physical manifestation within the body by tuning in to the Universal Life Force, rewiring our luminous energy and chakras. It is possible to activate dormant strands of DNA, turn off certain genes and activate others, opening doors to self-realization and the ability to create instant physical, emotional and spiritual transformation.

The Alto Mesalloqs, the highest level Paqos of the Peruvian Andes, known as the Masters of the Living Energy, live and breathe this reality every moment of their lives. Through gratitude, rituals and ceremonies, they are in a continual dialogue and energetic exchange, weaving the Celestial Light and Energy the Golden Age into this time-space continuum for the benefit of the Pacha Mama and all living beings. Vision involves a two-way process, an ingress or inward movement of light, and an outward projection of mental images. As the Light codes from the Golden Age enter an individual or group through a stream of consciousness, igniting new ideas, mindsets and attitudes, new paradigms and new a world can be birthed. The Frequencies of the Golden Age are available now for anyone to tap into, to start rewiring your energy fields with, and to become a living embodiment and template of The Golden Age. In turn a new morphogenic field begins to form and inform the collective.

Cleansing and fortifying the energy Field
In the Andean language there is no word for negative energy.

They view what we call negative energies, as hucha (hoo-cha). Hucha is dense, low vibrational energy that is neither good nor bad. It's just energy vibrating at a lower frequency. Sami (saw-mee) in the Quechua language is refined energy. Refined energy or sami has the ability to transmute hucha as we go through transformation and work to transmute the events, traumas and beliefs that produce hucha. The more sami or high vibrational energy we have running through us, the more effective we are going to be at transmuting our heavier energies. The Andean medicine person also views dark forces or dark energies in a person's life as a potential means of growth and evolution for that person. Much of the process is determined by the perspective the person holds and the amount of spiritual light that person has cultivated in their life.

Saminchakuy

Saminchakuy (saw-mi-cha-qui) is an elemental practice with the Andean tradition, used to michuy (mee-qui), or transmute hucha, and bring in qualities of sami for cleansing the energy field or a space. The first step is to connect with sami from the cosmos, celestial realms and the Light of Creator in the Hanaq Pacha (upper world), then to direct the downward flow of light of the living energy, asking it to saturate, surround and penetrate. If you are working with your personal energy field, you must open your energy body and energy channels within the body with breath and sound. While pulling sami down, focus your intention on bringing the sami to where you feel the hucha residing, and with your intention and exhale release the heavy energies downward, while asking the Mother Earth to receive and assist in transmuting the hucha. The energies of Puma and the element of fire can also be called up for this practice. Puma eats and transmutes the hucha and fire will burn and purify it. Not only are we going through our own transformation, which can result in the surfacing of stuck energy turned to hucha, but we are also constantly in interchange and exchange with other entities and in places where hucha has accumulated. I cannot express enough the importance of a daily saminchakuy practice to avoid the over accumulation of hucha and to stay healthy and vibrant.

The practice of Saminchakuy can also be used to build and fortify your energy, even when you're not feeling the specific need to release hucha. Pulling up sami energy from the Earth as well as pulling light down from the Sun and Cosmos you will be working with the opposing forces of creation, the principle of Yanantin (ya-nan-teen), bringing together and harmonizing, complimentary opposite energies. I do this practice at least once a day in the morning and if needed I'll do it several times throughout the day. Masintin (ma-seen-teen) is the practice of bringing together similar energies that are complimentary. Mapping the land and our lives to bring together all parts of the whole, opposing and similar, is the practice of weaving ourselves back into creation.

The birth places of the new era

Water and bodies of water, are and continue to be the most revered element in the Andean traditions. In the Andean cosmology it is the water from which all life was born. Similarly, In Hawaiian Huna, wai, meaning water, is also the source of life, abundance and resource. To say one is blessed or abundant in Hawaiian would be to say that one is waiwai. In ritual and in ceremony it is the water that flows from the Apus and from natural springs and openings in the pacha mama, known as pakarinas (paw-ka-reen-a) that is used for healing. Pakarinas are natural openings in the earth that appear as caves or holes that contain the essential aspect of creation. They are the birthplaces of creation. The places of emergence and convergence, where the chaotic, dark, and intangible aspects of life and the earth cosmology come together with the light. For the Inca and current Q'ero peoples it is the water that springs through the pakarinas that they love to use in ceremony, for cleansing and healing. Pakarinas are also considered gateways to the ukhu pacha (underworld) and therefore are entry points into the inner realms of the unconscious and forgotten memories of our connection to existence. When the waters of a pakarina are used in a healing ceremony a person is able to access the inner realms of consciousness with more ease. The spirit of the water opens the doorways to these inner realms and assists the seeker in their internal flow.

The Inca were masters of water. The systems they built to irrigate their lands and provide the community with fresh water are astounding. Throughout the Andes you will find that all the ruins were built with a series ceremonial baths and fountains. It was in these ceremonial sites that initiates went through purification. Water from the Apus, pakarinas, contain what the Q'ero refer to as Illya (eeh-ya). The healing power of water is contained within this element of Illya. Illya is the pre-manifest, un-potentiated, primal life force of creation and kausay is the manifest form of Illya. Illya contained within the sacred waters of rivers and underground springs, has the ability to shatter and transform denser energies held within the chakras and energy body, and is considered one the most powerful agents in nature, for clearing imprints, cleansing and re-imprinting a person with the primal energy of creation.

The Andean people live with the knowledge of their star heritage and that we all are children of the stars. In their cosmology it is the Pleiades that contain the map of our return home and the seeds of our becoming. The order of a new cosmology, the "Golden Age" of once again knowing and living in our divine perfection is written in the stars and held within the pakarinas. Hence, for the shaman it is essential to map the land where they live, to find the sacred pakarinas and develop a relationship with fertility, so creation can constantly come into order and express itself through her.

"While in ceremony we step out of linear time, beyond language and reasoning, and into the sacred, where true understanding, healing and wisdom reside. We step beyond the limitations of the mind and into the boundless potential where the Heart, Spirit and the forces of creation unite." Chandra Sun Eagle

Nuna

Everything in the Universe, collectively and individually, is animated by Spirit. This is the essence and universal law of Nuna. All life, small and large, the plants, trees, two legged, furred, winged ones, stones, stars and rivers are all infused with the essence of Spirit. In the Quechua language Creator or Great Spirit cannot be so easily defined by one or two words, or even three for that matter, as in the English language. When an Andean Paqo calls to the Creator there are ten or more words, all containing multi-layered meaning, to invoke and pray to Spirit and the Light of Creation that infuses all life. The ability to recognize Spirit manifested in everything allows us to create affinities with both our trans-temporal or eternal nature, and our temporal nature, and the ability to express our presence in the world as both.

The luminous marker of Nuna also denotes the ability to articulate the language of Spirit, the language of the sacred, in thought, in intent, in action, and in every aspect of life. Recognizing Spirit in all life connects us with the sacred thread of reverent consciousness that weaves through us and as us, creating a life of right action. Right action for the Paqo is always comes from being aligned with Spirit.

What most people see with their eyes is only 1% of reality. The other 99% is the world of spirit and the world of energy that is flowing through life and form on the Earth. The Paqo is in full awareness that it is the force of Spirit and the realms of the invisible that inform and create the physical world. And it is from this awareness that a natural response to be in full participation with Spirit, to live and create in sacred time, through ceremony is birthed. Life is lived as a ceremony. The life, sacred space and potency of the Andean Paqo or shaman is directly related to how much spiritual energy and harmonious relationship they have cultivated within them, within their bodies and their luminous energy field. The means by which they do this largely through ceremony and ritual. Their life is about cultivating and filling their inner world with the energy of Spirit and growing that spiritual energy within them. They understand that new life, beauty and wellbeing are born through them and from them, so they spend their lives developing a life force infused with the essence of Spirit, the elements, celestial and earth frequencies so that they become the vessel through which creation is birthed.

Andean spirituality and the shamanic path are a very embodied way of life. When Paqos go into other realms they enter through dances, chanting and drumming, breath and rhythm to bring them into luminous states of awareness. But equally important to the luminous state of awareness that is acquired, is the Paqo's empowerment to take their bodies and consciousness into other dimensions and bring the energy, information and wisdom gained from the journey, back into this realm and infuse their Earth Walk with it. To do this they first attune their inner wisdom or serpent essence, their conscious self and jaguar essence with their spiritual bodies and psychic senses. This state of alignment allows them to take all aspects of themselves, including their bodies into the other realms.

The Paqo's effectiveness on a desired outcome, to facilitate a healing, or to return vital life force to a person, the land, a home or a relationship is not so dependent on the outward methodologies, as it is on their state of unity with Source, their connection to the elements, the spirit world and the land. Spirit lives, expresses and speaks through everything, in every moment of life and sometimes in the most mysterious ways. The methods through which a Paqo works is only a part of the equation.

Opening to Nuna through ceremony

As mentioned above, ritual and ceremony are central to the Andean way of Life. They understand that ceremony and approaching life in a ceremonial manner, opens new pathways for the language of Spirit to inform us and our lives. Since the beginning of time it has been the creating of sacred space and the art of ceremony that has opened the doors of communication between the indigenous people and the spirit world and the spirit within all life. The act of ceremony was, and remains to this day, a space in which the medicine person is able to suspend the mind and enter the domain of the soul and the domain of the Great Mystery. It is in ceremonial space that we create offerings for the Mother Earth, the spirits and Great Spirit, in order to give back to life, seek guidance, and to bridge the worlds.

To make our life a ceremony is to recognize and honor the gift of life itself. A life of ceremony is a life of service to the sacred. I remember my first shamanic ceremonies like it was yesterday and to this day, every ceremony that I facilitate or participate in, takes me into the awe and magic of what life is about. Everything makes sense to me when I'm in ceremony, where the truth of reality exists and comes alive. I experience my full self, my true nature and know myself beyond all other knowing. Every time a shaman holds a ceremony, we drop our self-identity to become an open vessel, known as the hollow bone in Native American traditions, for Spirit and Universal forces to work through us and as us. We open doorways to other dimensions and travel through the heart of the Universe, into other realms to unify, harmonize and heal. Through ceremony we co-create beauty with supernatural powers so we can flower into our highest expression of life - to connect with the center of creation and the center of all our relations. It is through the sacred ceremonies that we discover the original instructions of Creator and natural law that have nothing to with man-made law or human translation. The journey of discovering and bringing to life my purpose has brought me through the initiations and trainings to carry and hold the sacred ceremonies my soul was and is so familiar with - The Despacho Ceremony, Transmutational Fire Ceremonies, The Sweat Lodge Ceremony, as well as the Master Plant Ceremonies of Ayahuasca and Huachuma (San Pedro).

To create ceremony is to create a space for Spirit to enter and fully express through us, to call forward and invite the Celestial Ones, Beings of Light, our Spirit Guides and animal allies into the space and into our lives. Through ceremony we are invoking the forces of nature and we are saying to the Spirit world that we recognize their presence in our lives, and we are there in that moment to commune, ask for help and to honor our connection with them. All ceremonies can be constructed, approached and conducted with different intentions, but should always be approached with humility, through the Heart and with the Highest Good For All Concerned in mind, first and foremost. During ceremony and ritual, we are inviting the spirit world into our life, and, at the same time, we are stepping into the realm of Spirit. It is a continuum of energetic presence and communication that flows both ways. Ceremony is a merging of the physical with the Spirit and it is a merging of the Human Heart with our Spirit Heart. The Heart of the Cosmos harmonizing with the Great Central Heart. When we go into ceremony, we have to leave our ego outside of the ceremony so that we can move into our heart and into gratitude. When we are in our heart we enter into a unified and harmonious state, and are able to shift our consciousness to commune and come from our inner Divinity. While in ceremony we speak from our heart, make offerings from our heart and we give gratitude from our heart. In cultivating and expressing gratitude life becomes a ceremony and we are able to live and create from our connection with Source and our own wisdom and divinity.

The Power of ceremony and Spirit

Ceremony and Spirit have the power to heal, to transmute, cleanse and lift heavy energy. Being in ceremony slows us down and moves us into a state of reciprocity - Ayni. Ceremony can reestablish vitality, right relationship with the nature beings, the land and the spirits, and through a ceremonial life, we are able to move into a deeper understanding of the natural flow of cycles and seasons, and thus the cycles and seasons within us. We also enter into to ceremony to help lift us out of the heaviness of everyday stresses and to shift our attention from the mundane to the Divine, at the same time recognizing that the Divine can flow through all the mundane aspects of life. By bringing our stresses and challenging circumstances to a ritual and ceremonial space, we are shifting our perspective from "life is stressful" to "honoring everything and all circumstances in our life", even the very difficult and often times confusing situations.

Shamanic ceremony and journeys are fully embodied and sensory filled, tangible experiences. It's a full body experience, which contrary to what many have learned, is where the magic is. Experiencing the magical qualities of life is not about having out of body experiences, but rather bringing the magic of Spirit into our physical existence. When we are fully embodied and in altered states of consciousness, we are able to hear with our invisible ears and to see with our hearts. It's our non-ordinary senses that may just help us thrive. For example, this is how the shamans communicate with the plants to learn what healing properties they possess, which plants are complimentary and how to administer them.

Some years ago, I was facilitating a workshop in the healing ceremonies and ritual arts of the Andes. We were working with the Alchemical Fire Ceremony, the Andean Despacho Ceremony, Harnessing Energy from the Elements, Water Cleansing rituals and shamanic journeys to meet and commune with allies in the spirit, animal and plant world. On the evening of the first day we had just come out of a ceremonial journey into the plant world to connect with our personal plant allies, when I noticed that one of the women in the circle had both hands over her heart and tears were streaming down her face. I approached her softly and asked if she was ok. Shedding tears of joy and disbelief she told me of a rare disease that she'd contracted that had taken away her sense of smell years prior. For more than five years she had not been able smell anything, nothing at all. She then pointed to the palo santo burning in the smudge bowl and said in a quiet voice, "It has come back. I can smell. During the journey I met the spirit of the sage plant and it told me my ability to smell would come back. I can't believe it. How did that happen?"

Astonished and in awe we listened to her story and watched as she, one by one, picked up various organic items from the altar and tenderly inhaled the essence with deep reverence. Not only had her sense of smell returned but a sense of wonder and hope also returned to her life. She left the workshop with a new level of trust in the mystery of life. A couple of months later I received a gift in the mail and an accompanying letter from her. Ceremony had become a regular part of her life. Her renewed sense of smell brought with it a new gift, an opening to an extra-sensory skill. Through smell, she said, she could now actually hear the voice of the flower or plant she was touching. She told me that a profound level of communication and relationship to the plant world had opened for her after that weekend, and was guiding her to study flower essences, essential oils and vibrational healing. She was beyond ecstatic. It was a miracle.

A new phase of creation

Ceremony brings us into unity. We are at the beginning of a new phase of creation and awakening, the Taripay pacha. The Pachakuti, the turning over of a cycle, has brought us into a time of purification and transition, with waves of higher frequencies pulsing from the Universe. These waves of high frequency energies are constantly hitting us and are encouraging us to pray, to cleanse, and move into the high heart, consciously bringing gratitude for the blessings of this new phase of awakening. Within this transition, we each have a responsibility to participate consciously and to assist with the "human family" awakening. Awakening will shift us out of being drained and stressed by what's happening. So that we can become full of vitality and well-being. This is possible. And the energies of new life and well-being are always available to us. Doing our ceremonies, the releasing and cleansing ceremonies, along with dreaming ceremonies will assist us greatly during these transformational times.

As the higher frequencies from the cosmos flow to the planet and through us, the energies that are not in resonance with the Golden Age will be illuminated, disrupted and agitated. It's our job to recognize these patterns and energies, to work with them consciously and bring them to ceremony. The process of transmutation that has to occur is happening. The fire of transmutation and purification is burning, and it is happening now for everyone, all over the world, whether they choose to recognize it as such or not. No one is exempt from the process we are going through. For those not wanting to awaken or not wanting to change, this will be an even more challenging time. Spirit is calling to once again be recognized as the primary directive of Life and the voice of Mother Earth is speaking in unison. We can choose ease in our awakening or we can choose the hard way. Shamans are always praying for the gentlest path to healing and transformation. From the Andean perspective even when we are experiencing a very challenging situation in life, we give thanks, we bring love to the situation. We recognize this must be what we need and things could often be much worse. Ceremony helps us to see and tap into other solutions to our problems and challenges. Taking our doubts, stresses and anger to ceremony can help ease our worried minds and lighten the heart. Ceremony opens new pathways for the language of Spirit to inform us and our lives. Life is magical, even during these times, but those not wanting to wake up miss out on the beauty available to them. They miss out on the opportunity to grow and evolve. Going into ceremony brings us into the magic and vibration of love, as well as into other states of consciousness. Revitalizing our soul and energy body in ceremonial ways during this Shift of the Ages is critical, and is a way to fully participate in our personal and collective transformation.

Waking up from hundreds of years of virus programming that tells us that we are separate from the Divine, is critical. Outer acts of ceremonies and offerings wake up the sacred and Spirit within us, putting us in touch with our being as a spiritual light, who we are beyond our body, beyond our skin. We are part of this miracle of life. We arrived here on this earth like shooting stars. Become conscious of this miracle. There are powerful forces that are trying to block us and limit our self-love and potential. Shamanic ceremony is so essential to helping us remember our true nature and that Spirit resides in all life. Each morning, Paqos and medicine people all over the world, stand before the rising sun and breathe in the blessings, possibilities and light of the new day, while offering themselves to the sacred. They set the tone of the day by realizing their inner sun and inner fire are fed by the infinite potential carried through the Light of Tata Inti, Father Sun.

From the Andean perspective we are always in an evolutionary process and within this process, we have great assistance from the Ancestral Lineages that have left this physical plane. In their ceremonies, coca leaf readings and journeying they always connect with the wisdom and power of their lineage because those ancestors are no longer touched by doubts, fears or separation and so they offer us connection to the ancient living wisdom of truth and power in the now.

The Next Seven Generations

As a collective, becoming conscious of what kind of world and atmosphere we are creating for our children and the next seven generations is imperative. Is it one where the Spirit within all is recognized and honored?

Pullkay (pooh - kie), is Quechua for the innocence of sacred play and is how they approach their lives. The Andean people involve and teach their children from an early age about the sacredness of life. The children are shown how to tend the seeds of their future through sacred play and are involved in ceremony and assist in the ceremonies from a very early age in the Andes. I love this word pullkay so much. It reconnects me with the inner wisdom of my childlike essence and invites that part of me to be present and bring my joy, even in the most serious of times. In our society many of the young seeds of the world are not being tended to. Instead, children are burdened by having to become over achievers just to get into the right pre-school. From an early age they are attacked by the forces self-doubt, comparison, stress and imbalance so prevalent in our society. Introducing children to playful ceremony and ritual can show them how to release these tensions and stresses. We need to take care of their innocence. Children absorb everything around them and in their environment. By bringing them into ceremony they can absorb the beauty and the power of ceremony, the feeling of hope and connectedness to Spirit. It will give them other tools besides education to help them bloom and grow into their best selves. Reverence for life is an organizing principle from the beginning of life in the Andes. Ceremony has most certainly done this for me and the hundreds of people I've worked with.

Moving into a ceremonial space with life our perceptions and our understanding expands. A ceremonial mindset and attitude are open, humble, connected and strengthen our ability to navigate change and adapt to life's challenges with grace. We gain more understanding of what our life is teaching us by seeing what is showing up through a different lens. Otherwise, everything we are dealing with will continue to loop and cycle back around.

I encourage you to create more beauty and invite Spirit into your life and the life of your family and community by designing and performing more ceremonies that celebrate the sacred. And remember, the more joy you bring to it the more power you will experience.

Andean Despacho Ceremony

The central ceremony of exchange, healing and harmonizing in the Andes is known as the Despacho Ceremony. The ceremony is an act of love, an act of Ayni. There are many types of despachos, most commonly created as a ritualistic offering to the Pachamama or to the Apu kuna (mountain spirits). Despachos are also ceremonial offerings created for healing, for life transitions, to bring harmony between a person and their family or community, to weave our presence and connection into a unified state with creation and the three worlds, and to align our inner vision with the sacredness of life and its highest expression. Ceremonial ingredients such as coca leaves, grains, seeds, nuts, herbs, chocolates and sweets, flowers, incense, spices, red and white wine, feathers, silver, gold and rainbow-colored threads, symbolically representing all aspects of creation, are infused with prayer and with soulful intent. Through the essence and breath of the Paqo, each ingredient and each participant's desires are woven into the offerings, and placed carefully on piece of paper or natural fiber, in a mandala of prayer. The despacho is then wrapped in a tight bundle, passed over the person's energy field as part of the cleansing process of old or stuck energies, and then either brought to a sacred fire for burning or placed in earth.

I've been a part of and have performed numerous despacho

ceremonies over the past 17 years. Each one has been different and just as beautiful as the others. It is the work of the Andean Paqo to master this ceremony. And although this is a brief description of the ceremony, I share this as a seed of intention that you incorporate some type of ceremonial offering on a regular basis in your life.

Don't hesitate! Delay no longer!

Make your life a sacred ceremony!

"We each contain within us the Seed of Love. Love is our origin, the nectar of life and the greatest healing power there is."
Chandra Sun Eagle

Munay

Munay (moon-eye) is impersonal, unconditional, timeless love, the fabric that binds all life. For the Andean Paqo, Munay is Absolute Truth, through which all thought and action must align. Truth is a frequency of God Light and the Andean Paqo recognizes that without Truth, Munay is not present in its fullest, truest essence. There cannot be Absolute Love without the integrity of Absolute Truth. Munay therefore is Love, beyond the expression of romantic love. Munay is the quality of the timeless, all compassionate, unconditional and impersonal love that weaves together everything in the universe. Munay establishes that love is the fundamental affinity and bridge that brings together all levels of consciousness. It is the connective tissue that integrates the three worlds, and it is the bridge that frees us from judgments, our suffering, consensual imprints of fear and separation, and it is the bridge that frees us from our egos. Munay is what awakens us to living in heart-centered communication and in alignment with unity-consciousness. It is what allows us to move into acceptance and gratitude for all that is.

The guide stone of Munay is the binder that holds all together in the Universe and guides the spiritual initiate into higher states of Love based consciousness and Truth.

The heart center, (sonqo in Quechua), is the primary energy center through which the Andean people engage reality, and access Cheka, the absolute truth about one's past, present and future becoming. It is the bridge to realizing one's transcendent, trans-temporal and essential nature. Enfolded within the heart's wisdom, are the keys to harmony, peace and abundance. The heart is where the ancients have been telling us to focus our attention and to align our intentions. They tell us that the heart is the Central Sun within our energy body and it contains the power to purify and transform anything.

Munay is essential to and at the center of life in the Andean Culture. Everything and every moment of their lives is approached through the heart, through unconditional love. This is the manner in which they tend and take care of their children, the land, the animals, the innocence and purity of life. Living in Munay results in a conscious connection and communication with our high self and it is through the high self that miracles and instantaneous healing happens. We all have an inner spring of Love that flows naturally when we remove doubt, fear, judgment, guilt and shame. When our heart is full with love and joy of the cosmos it leaves no room troubling energies. It is common in today's world, especially in the circles of spiritual seekers, for most people to agree that Love is the answer to fear, that Love is the path to peace, to happiness, and the key to a life of fulfillment. But how do we get from the concept of Love to becoming an embodiment of Love? What is the experience of Love in our lives? WE must look at our living experience of love. With honesty and self-transparency we have to undertake self-inquiry and look at how the qualities of love, like patience, acceptance, gratitude, kindness, forgiveness, and non-judgment are expressed in our relationship to ourselves, in our familial relationships, our friendships, towards our mother earth, the animals, the environment, our neighbors and those we cross paths with as we go through our day. Being transparent and truthful with ourselves, while examining these questions, provides a simple and sustainable practice to see clearly what degree Munay is alive within us. Our High Self, the aspect of our soul that is Pure Love Consciousness, is our guardian angel. It is the part of us that has extended a thread of Light from its golden essence down into this plane of existence to connect with our elemental self and conscious self. Conscious communication and connection with our high self is a direct link to experiencing the Love from which we were born and which we are. Love is not something outside of us, but we do have to invite and give permission to our High Self to guide us and intervene when it's in our highest good. Every human being has free will which cannot be over ridden, even by our own High Self, unless we have consciously given it permission to intervene when are about to do something against ours or someone else's highest good and well-being.

Love is at the core of our highest nature and is the most powerful force in the Universe. Love is the greatest protection and the most assured path to Liberation. Beginning, of course, with revolutionary Self Love, accepting and loving all aspects of oneself back into wholeness. For without the embodiment of Self Love, one is not prepared nor can truly understand how to love others from a higher state of unconditional love, with compassion and truth. Many people in our world did not and do not grow up in an environment of unconditional love. Nor have they learned the art of love for life, and are afflicted with the psychological and physical manifestations of that lack of love. Many have negative experiences imprinted within their emotional and mental bodies. And because of this there is most likely a limited comfort level to which they are willing to feel and to open. The discomfort or a deep fear of revisiting and feeling the emotions associated with past events creates a tendency to suppress, ignore or block a significant amount of our potential life force, and ability to live with clear communication and creative impulse. When feelings are suppressed or dissociated from, life force (kausay), and the frequency at which the person vibrates, decreases. When the vibrational frequency of your energy body is diminished, so is your physical strength, your mental clarity, the function of your immune system and the passion you feel for life. The emotions you are afraid to feel and the events you are afraid to face ultimately are what hold you back from experiencing the fullness of life, and from entering the magnetic power of the heart.

If you are the one that has acted in non-loving ways, it is imperative to ask for forgiveness from the person and to forgive yourself. If not, suffering is created by the feelings of guilt and regret, and thoughts of 'if only I had been kind", "I feel so bad, I should not have done or said that", which, if not resolved, end up committed to the memory bank and feedback loop of the subconscious. Fear itself, fear of feeling fear, fear of the unknown, fear of being vulnerable, fear of being rejected, fear of being outcast or not accepted, fear of making mistakes, all live within the minds and hearts of humankind. The consensual reality is saturated with it. It is a projection of negative imprinting and it is an illusion. As we all know, fear is also a tool that has been used to weaken and divide, and is used by many as means to gain control and attain wealth. From fear comes many negative acts. Fear immobilizes and dis-empowers. Are you ready to move out of fear, out of illusion and into Truth, into the freedom of residing in Munay, love?

Weaving a new world with the threads of Love

Mystics and shamans know that everything that manifests in the physical world exists first as a seed of potential in the spiritual world and within the quantum field of possibilities. The world we live in is a myriad of individual and collectively agreed upon projections. Our immediate reality and the expanded world reality are always mirroring back to us what we have created and are recreating on an individual and collective level.

It is time to dream a new dream - to place our attention more acutely on what is resonating within us and who we are on a vibrational level before taking action in the world. Our focus should be attuned to who we are becoming and energetically how we are showing up in our lives. More than what we are doing in the world, is the energy with which we are creating. The higher quality of Munay that we are vibrating, the more coherent impact our actions will have on our world. If our energy is split due to a misalignment in our energy field and consciousness, our actions will create the same energetic misalignment. Take for example the one who is preaching Love and words of the scriptures in the name of God, yet holds judgement and condemns those who do hold the same beliefs or lives their life according to his way. What is energetically being projected through their actions is not of true love.

In today's western world there is a considerable interest on what we need or what we can get. I witness this mindset of lack and selfishness overshadowing the potential of spiritual growth and evolution in many people. True happiness and a life lived in Munay and in Ayni, is not about what we can get from or get back from the world, but rather what and how we give and offer to this world. The dial of our inner compass is ready to be oriented toward the magnetic north of gratitude, what we leave to this world and how we can offer our lives in service to humanity, the children of the next seven generations, the animals and this glorious earth we have the privilege to walk upon. When offering ourselves, our voices and actions in the name of Munay, our path will become clear, our life and most meaningful existence will be motivated by the impulses our highest nature.

Something very magical happens inside when you decide to embrace the way of the Heart. Your very existence takes on new meaning. You will no longer look to the material world or the outside world for validation, or to fill any emptiness or loneliness. Embracing the Path of the Heart places you in a field of new perception and grace that alters how you see and view everything in your life and around you. Remember, everything is energy. Every thought, belief, memory and emotion contain the energy that creates your life. The moment you change your perception you change your life. A devotional life to the path of Munay places you in a stream of higher frequencies and an inner condition where love for all life becomes an organizing principle, where the gift of enlightenment and the blessing of living in a perpetual state of grace is attainable. In the Andean tradition the one who reaches this state has achieved what is called "Munayniyok" (moon-eye-knee-yolk), the one who is Love, has Love and gives Love.

Love provides us the strength and awareness needed for navigating all of lives circumstances. It is the strongest purifier and most powerful harmonizer. Love is the rope we hold onto to rise through all states of existence in order to return home to the Heart of the Universe. When Love is placed as the central pillar in your life, you will become very magnetic and a potent source of attraction. Your soul will be fed with the sweetest elixir, giving you the nourishment needed to make it through discouraging or painful times in life. All levels of your soul will blossom into their eternal nature and state of unity, becoming the flower and fountain of Love, from which all life can drink and miracles can flow. Wisdom and Truth are shown to those who reside in the state of Munay. Joy, happiness and fulfillment are the rewards. Those seeking pathways and solutions that lead to the well-being of all life, not just the well-being of self, will find themselves in an eternal flow of abundance. Love is the power to overcome darkness, and make the impossible, possible. It is the key to All things Great!

As mentioned earlier, Munay is a frequency of Truth. Munay is not blind nor does it whitewash the shadowy behaviors of oneself or others. A common statement I hear is "it's all good". This statement, more often than not, comes from a person that wants to stay in a "feeling" of love, but actually holds judgement or feels hurt from another person or situation and is not being honest. They either don't want to admit these feelings within themselves or don't know what to do with the feelings, so they jump to the statement of "it's all good", when in fact it is not. They've just leapt over what needs addressing. This leads to denial, lying to oneself and/or whitewashing the behaviors of others or ourselves. It takes a lot of energy to cover up how we truly feel and to hide what we don't want others to see about us. Similarly, it takes a lot of energy to hide from ourselves what we wish not to see about another, resulting in a world of false niceties, masks and shallow connections. One of my teachers explained it like this. We are living in a world where a large portion of humanity is living within the confines of an unspoken agreement. That agreement says something to this affect, "I won't touch your wounds if you don't touch mine" and "I won't point out what makes you uncomfortable if you do the same for me." Keeping each other blind and in an illusory state of "comfortability" is the result, with a whole treasure chest of impurities bubbling just under the surface, growing into large monsters that eventually find their way to the surface.

Another misconception I come across often is the Illusion that to love means that we have to be everyone's best friend if we are truly a good spiritual person. Not true. Remember that the essence of Munay contains within it the frequency of Truth and the truth is, is that we are not going to resonate or agree with everyone. And that is ok. But what must be done is to move the experience and our perception of that person to a higher perspective of a non-judgmental acceptance, and then bless the situation with Munay. It's important to be open to the views of others and to not get locked into thinking our way is the right way or the only way, this is where judgement sneaks in through the back door.

In the Andes the people know themselves as the Children of the Sun or Children of the Light. What does it mean to know oneself as a Child of the Sun or Child of the Light? Within the Andean is the experience and understanding that they, and all of us came into this physical world as an emanation of the Light of Creator. Deep within them, there is a knowing that we come from the Love of Creator and that we are held by the Love of the Pacha Tata, the cosmic father and Pacha Mama, the Cosmic Mother, throughout our life here on Earth. From this knowing arises an innate understanding that our lives are blessed and that life is a blessing. When we continue to draw the Light of Creator, from which we were born, into our lives, into our hearts and energy bodies, Light can express through and as us more freely and powerfully. Light can flow unimpeded and when Light is flowing freely the potential for turning an ordinary life into extra-ordinary life grows and accelerates. We are a ray of Light and with Light there is clarity, and purity. There is life and there is transparency. Our origins and original nature are one of Light. Inside each of us is our own Sun. For the Andean Paqo this Sun within is inextricably One with the Great Sun and Light of Creator. Within our inner sun, is contained the seed of Creator, but many people in the West have forgotten this and have forgotten the source from which they come. They have slipped far away from their origins and truest essence. Their connection to Light, to Spirit and to their High Self has been compromised, and in some cases severely damaged. This does not mean the wounding is permanent or that the person cannot heal and restore their connection.

During this time of great purification, transformation and awakening, there is a tremendous amount of contrast and duality present in our reality. However, the extreme contrast is allowing us to see clearly in our lives and in our world, what has detracted from the living energy of Munay and Light. Mystics, the world over, are saying that, more than ever before, the cosmos pushing and supporting us to awaken to the true nature of Light that we are. When we truly embody that Light, we change our perception of our life, of the life around us and new meaning emerges.

The power of forgiveness

So, how does one find their way back into Munay, with themselves and the Light within? An understanding of where the roots and origins of blockages, fears, hurts, traumas and experiences of the past must be discovered. How do we make our way back into the truest essence of Love from which our souls were originally created?

To come back into Munay and establish residence in the great cosmic sun within, there is much healing, forgiveness and peacemaking to do. We must each bring harmony to our past, to our history and to our traumas that have happened and continue to create heaviness, sadness and depression in our lives, and the myriad of coping mechanisms to avoid the aforementioned. These imprints that did not originate from love become the blockages to us experiencing who we truly are, unless we learn to forgive and use the events of the past as springboard to catapult us toward the Light.

Mystics have been telling us for thousands of years that Love is what truly heals. Words, intentions and actions devoid of unconditional love do not heal. It is the energy of non-dualistic Love behind our words and actions that is the most powerful of healing forces.

The extent of our mission to release the heavy energies of the past, to forgive ourselves and others is immeasurable in its effect on reality. Bringing forgiveness to our past, brings clarity to our past and harmonizes the energies so that we can begin to create a different relationship to our past story, and a different reality. When our energies are harmonized with Munay and our inner sun, we become like a crystal that refracts rays of light. We become luminous and in each of those rays we are able to bring forward our gifts and talents to add to the spectrum of life and creation. We are able to contribute to the evolution of life in the way of beauty, of joy and peace. We are able to grow spiritually and help others grow spiritually. It is each of our responsibility to bring our best self forward in life. Because we are Children of the Light and Children of Love, when we harmonize our life, we in turn help harmonize our planet. This too, is part of our mission.

It is very important to recognize the light within us and to make sure that our thoughts and actions are coming from that inner light and heart. Like the Sun that brings light and warmth to life on Mother Earth, we must invite this Light into us. Every day we have to practice bringing Light from the cosmic father and cosmic mother into our minds, into bodies, into our emotions. We need to do practices of feeding our ourselves the Light of Creation and awakening even more the Sun within. Living from the inner light and the qualities of Munay with all expressions of life, no matter what the situation, we have the power to transform an ordinary life into an extraordinary life. On the contrary, with the absence of Munay, there is an absence of flow, there is dryness, and our souls become weak, and we fall prey to a life of inauthenticity, a life of ego. Make the commitment to transform your life and return to your essence. Have the courage to look at yourself honestly and see what types of energies you are contributing to this world. Stop placing blame and take responsibility. Become aware that your reaction or experience of an event is based on your interpretation, your own projection and creation of it. Realign yourself with Munay, the Light of Absolute Truth.

During the past century the western world has been giving so much attention to the power of the mind in relation to creating new technologies. We have and continue to create new technologies every day. But where are most of these technologies guiding us? For many, they are guiding us, and our children deeper into the mind of media, video games and computers, and further away from the earth and our connection to nature, thus they are guiding us further away from ourselves. I am not saying that technology is bad or the cause of our problems. I'm simply pointing out the obvious. Most people are way out of balance between the heart and the mind, the natural world and the material world. We are teaching and further perpetuating the belief that we can only create with our mind and that reality is based in the material world.

Science is proving what the Ancients have always known

As spoken about in the chapter on kausay, yachay, munay and llankay are the three primary principles of exchange and the exchange centers, within the energy body, through which the Andean Paqo engages life. A quick reminder, yachay is the power of knowledge, educating ourselves and maintaining right thinking, awakening primal life energy and raising it in consciousness. Munay is the power to engage life through the heart and unconditional love. When yachay and munay are fully awakened and embodied, llankay, our service and action, in the world is aligned with our higher centers of the mind and our hearts. Our service and actions then become spontaneously free and unlimited in their potential. A Lokata elder once told me the longest walk we humans would ever make in this life time was the walk from the mind to the heart. Sad, but true I thought to myself, as I looked around, through my mind's eye, at the state of the world and proliferation of war and destruction of our natural world.

A research group at the Institute of HeartMath, in Boulder Creek, California, have discovered that the heart has its own brain, a real brain with actual brain cells. It was discovered we have within our hearts about 40,000 specialized cells called sensory neurons. These sensory neurons are much like the neurons in our brain, but they learn, feel and experience independently from the cells in our brain. The function of these heart cells is to learn, think and remember differently, making our heart a memory bank of its own with its own intelligence.

And these cells in the heart can be harmonized with those in the brain! When the heart and brain harmonize in a coherent state, neurological pathways to our super powers activate. For instance, our intuition and higher learning centers are easily accessed, our immune system gets stronger, our body's innate healing powers turn on, anti-aging hormones are produced and higher states of joy and feeling good are felt immediately. Intuition is heightened. Learning accelerates and the potential for memory becoming acutely accurate is possible. We can have total recall of something we've learned or experienced. The Heart Brain harmonization and communication becomes a conduit and direct access to our subconscious, where these memories and events are stored.

Science has also discovered that the greatest conversation occurs between the heart and the brain. It is bigger than the conversation that happens from the brain to the spinal cord. The brain first receives instructions from the heart. Then the brain releases the chemistry. The quality of the conversation and messages from the heart is what tells the brain which chemicals to release. When the heart is sending negative emotional messages such as fear, anger, frustration, or jealousy the electrical pulses and waves from the heart are very jagged, a set of stress hormones are released from the brain that then send our body into a learned response of either fight, flight or freeze. Continued and repeated production of stress hormones, over time, keep us in heightened states of stress, that over tax our adrenals, immune systems, and eventually the passion for life. Life becomes a continual struggle. When the heart is sending positive and coherent feelings, images and messages, a completely different set of hormones is released that bring us into a feeling of vitality and peace. So, when we practice Munay, compassion, unconditional love, and gratitude the hormones released from the brain produce an immediate response that would be considered a healed state. The ancients knew this and the Andean Paqos still live this. It's evident in their way of life, in their rituals and ceremonies. They just don't use science to explain it.

An equally amazing discovery, by this same research group, is that the heart generates the largest and most powerful energy field of any organ in the body, including the brain within the skull. They found that the heart's electromagnetic field is about eight to ten feet in diameter, with the axis centered in the heart. Its shape resembles the donut form of a torus, which is often considered the most unique and primal shape in the universe and is the shape of energy flowing around the Earth. This same institute has spent years, conducting controlled experiments that resulted in some fascinating findings. The studies pointed to the potential for humans to clean the environment with the power of their light body. When we create with our thoughts and our hearts as a unified cohesive unit, through our medicine body, while staying connected to the Pacha Mama and the highest good, anything is possible. When we create from unity consciousness, we are doing what we were meant to do, to be caretakers and stewards of this beautiful planet.

We as humans stand between the worlds. We stand, breathe and live at the crossroads between the heavens and the earth, between the unseen and seen, with the potential to mediate these un-manifest and manifest realms of reality. Actually, beyond potential to mediate, is the fact that we are, in every moment of our life, mediating these forces through our thoughts, where we place our attention, our emotional reactions, the choices we make and the actions we consciously or unconsciously engage in. This is of utmost importance to understand. From this understanding we begin to shift our mode of creating, and we awaken within us the eternal flame of creation and an unbound passion for life. We are, without question responsible for the world we create. This is the truth of what the ancients have been trying to get us to awaken to. I often say that without the indigenous people, their ceremonies and ways of life, the web of our reality would be much more distorted than it has become. The very fabric of creation is woven and held together through their ceremonial lives and reciprocal exchanges with creation. In the current day, advancement and the over application of certain technologies is disrupting the electromagnetic field of the Earth and the biosphere. Weather patterns have become extreme and erratic. Life everywhere is experiencing the destructive effects of a technological age and the abuses of mankind. Where would we be without the life affirming and life sustaining ways of the ancients? Would the fabric of life be ripped apart by ignorance and egocentric entitlement? Quite possibly.

At the center of our energy body is our heart. It is the 4th chakra from our base chakra and lies between the upper three chakras, usually associated with the upper world and etheric realms, and the lower three chakras, most associated with the lower world and the earthly realms. Combine this ancient wisdom with the new found scientific knowledge of the vibrational power that the heart generates, and herein lies the key to creating harmony and beauty within and therefore without. Dreaming and bringing forth a new world of peace from the aftermath of religious and world wars, over consumerism, can seem impossible and futile when approached from the mind, but when approached from the heart, anything is possible.

The mind creates by using thoughts, and thoughts follow one another using logic. And so, whatever the mind creates, you can logically follow the path of how the reality has been transformed from one state to another. It will always generate both sides of the polarity of the original intention. The heart, however, works through a completely different realm of reality. The heart creates through dreams and images, and these manifest through feelings and emotions. This form of creation does not use logic and therefore does not have to be logical to get from one state to another. For example, if you are praying for rain through the heart, it could start raining immediately, even if there were no clouds in the sky only moments before. As mentioned earlier, and which I think is worth mentioning again, is that we all have within us a spring of Love that will flow abundantly and unimpeded, when we clear the doubt, the shame, guilt, anger and judgment. It's our own personal spring of love that is independent from any and all outside circumstances. This spring of natural love is the love from the cosmos for all life and it is the expression of Creator within our inner being, the Divine. To be in the natural flow of Munay is to be this Love, and then extend it to all life through caring for and nurturing the life around us.

Awakening the eternal flame of munay

After a few years of working with the Paqos and training in traditions of the high Andes I received the call to travel to the Amazonian Jungle of Peru to work with the sacred medicine and master plant teacher, Ayahuasca. It was here that another level of remembering of who I am, the source from which I was born, and the profound Truth of Munay was awakened.

Following a couple of weeks in the Sacred Valley and trekking to two Apus, Ausangate and Q'olloriti, a good friend and I spent a few days resting in Cusco and then took a flight to Puerto Maldonado. From there we hopped into a small motor boat with a few others and made our way up the Madre de Dios, river of the Southern Amazon. The warm humid air was welcoming after being in the dry arid climate of 14,000 feet. As the boat hummed along, I watched the beauty of the lush landscape slowly pass by and contemplated the intentions that had drawn me to the Amazon. Ayahuasca, or vine of the soul, is considered a master healer and teacher, always ingested in a ceremonial container, held by a well trained and experienced shaman, known as an Ayahuasquero. Adherence to proper spiritual and physical preparation prior to the ceremony is a must. The ceremony should be approached with great respect and the proper mind set. Ayahuasca is revered for its truth revealing properties and ability to take us into the crevices of our psyche, and soul that hold keys to our healing and awakening, often requiring a dying of sorts, a dying to illusion and beliefs of false education. Ayahuasca is un-compromising in her teachings and her command of respect, for her and for yourself. The plant had come to me in my dreams several times over the past months. Showing herself as large cosmic serpent amongst jungle scenes and brilliant colors that left me with a strong urge to make a journey to the jungle. And so, although not a typical part of the Andean Spiritual Path, I could not ignore the loud and consistent call from this most respected master. My intention? To show up fully in an open state and allow the messages of the one who had summoned me my full presence. And, if I could be shown the greater meaning to life that would be wonderful. I say that lightly, but it most certainly was a question I'd been searching the answer to.

By mid afternoon we reached the jungle resort and were lying on our beds listening to the orchestration of insects and jungle sounds. Everything was speaking and pulsing with life around us. The late afternoon and evening hours passed slowly, but the time to make our way to the beach on the other side of the Amazon finally arrived. Standing before us was the ayahuasquero and his apprentice, both wearing warm grins and back packs in hand. The ayahuasquero came highly recommended by a teacher, so I felt in good hands.

"Listas senoritas?" he asked, while extending a hug to us both. My friend and I exchanged a quick glance, lifted ourselves from the wooden bench and followed our guide down the dark path that lead to the river. Little butterflies flitted around in my stomach. The moon was full, but she had not yet risen. Darkness surrounded us except for the light of our headlamps that lit the windy path down to the river. I carefully placed one foot in front of the other staying close behind our guide. Just before reaching the river's edge something unusual happened. An energy rose out of the water and entered my body. It was a pleasant feeling and lasted only a few seconds, but once the energy left my body, I felt a great sense of calm, my nervousness had been washed away. I offered a silent prayer of gratitude and climbed into the small riverboat with the other three.

Once on the other side of the river, the ayahuasquero and his assistant built a small fire and instructed us to sit down in front of it. We sat across from one another and stared into the flames while the shaman offered Florida water, incenses and other items to the land and to the spirits. Walking in a circle around us, he spoke prayers and made more offerings in exchange for keeping us protected, for a deep healing ceremony, and a successful journey. From his powerful prayer I was already feeling altered. After a few more minutes, one at a time, the ayahuasquero came to each of us. Smoking tobacco and whistling softly, he blew the smoke into my hands and feet first, then down my back and down my front. The final blow went directly into the crown of my head. He did the same to my friend, to his assistant and then to himself.

Whistling a melodic tune, he opened the bottle of ayahuasca and blew the sacred tobacco into it. Raising the container to the heavens, down to the Earth and to his heart in between each blow. Offerings seemed to be complete for the moment as he poured the brown liquid into a cup. It was time to drink. My heart sped up a little as he handed me the small cup filled with the dark, thick medicine. He motioned for me to blow my essence into the cup before drinking and then tilted his head back and said "to do", all of it. And so, I did as instructed; lifted the cup to my lips, and drank it all in two big gulps. Wheeewww!! Bracing myself as the sludgy consistency of our mother ayahuasca made her way past my lips and into my stomach.

Ayahuasca is a purification ceremony and one should be ready to be cleansed on all levels and in all directions. In, out, up, down, sideways and backwards. It's all part of it. The trick is to keep it in long enough for the medicine to take effect. It took a few minutes, but the more I breathed into my body and stomach, the medicine gradually settled. I sat by the fire a while longer until the ayahuasquero told me to lie down and wait for the visions.

The night was calm and the stars were bright. I began to pray, "Pacha Mama, sweet mother earth, hold me in your arms tonight as I descend into your belly. When fear appears please show me the origin of this fear so I may let it go. Be with me Pacha Mama. Thank you, Pacha Mama." I prayed to the spirits of the land and to the spirit of ayahuasca. I asked that my resistances be shed so I could be one with the medicine. Stating my intention to touch and understand the meaning of life, the Absolute, I prayed for the clarity needed to recognize all else for what it is and to let it go. As I continued my prayers, I watched the stars above, and slowly, as the medicine took hold, the physical world around me began to pulsate as energy. The stars overhead grew in number and in size, and in luminosity, until there was only one massive star in the entire sky. Then that one star burst back into a thousand pieces, and the whole process would start over. First growing in number, growing in size, until their edges met and became one star. Then exploding back out into the dark sky in a multitude of expressions. I watched this for a while until my eyes got heavy and I heard the voice of the ayahuasquero tell me to close them. "Go inside," he said, and then he began to rattle and sing a jungle song known as an icaro. Icaros are medicine songs sung to invoke particular energies, power animals or spirits, to cleanse a person's energy field, or reconnect them with aspects of creation. As he sang, I directed my attention inward. Arms close at my sides, with hands folded over my belly, I noticed that my fingers were drawn into a tight ball, like I was desperately holding on to something. Letting go is difficult as everything around you begin to fall away. The tiny crickets I heard earlier, now sounded like giants. The cackle of the wild monkeys that was faint in the distance when we first arrived on the beach, grew louder and louder, as if they were coming closer to partake in the ceremony. The earth rolled and undulated beneath my spine. I could hear faint voices of several people and flashes of unknown faces sped by at lightning speed. Feeling like everything, known and unknown, was activating, all that appeared before me came as a flood of images and sensations. Slowing my breath, I relaxed into the embrace of the Mother Earth, and held steady with my prayer. This helped slow the influx of energy to steady streams of geometric colored patterns that were profoundly soothing to my entire being. A small child with dark skin and black hair came and sat next to me. His presence was comforting. He sang in language I didn't know, and from his song came pictures. Pictures of my life. Swallowed whole by a whirlpool of past emotions, I was taken into a hall of memories. Times when I had been made fun of by other children. Times as teenager when I felt awkward and out of place, self-doubt pervading. Memories of boys making fun of my developing breasts and athletic thighs, a prelude to years of being self-conscious. I had no idea these memories still held such a charge of emotion. A deep compassion for myself welled up from within as I watched the scenes roll by. Tears of grief rolling down my cheeks, I apologized to the young girl and young woman within. "I'm so sorry. You are so beautiful. I love you." I repeated to myself over and over. As the love and compassion for myself grew in my heart, my little girl came toward me, wrapped her arms around me and we became one. A light from within began to grow. It got brighter with each prayer. I felt like I was one big smile. My attention was then brought back to the undulating earth beneath me as it slowed and the ground beneath began to solidify. I was back on top. Back on top of the earth. The jungle's breath still moving through me. I relaxed and heard a voice say, "See all else for what it is." Breathing with my surroundings I could hear the ayahuasquero starting to rattle again. Just as quickly as I had come back to the physical reality of the jungle, I was swept away by another current of geometric patterns and sucked through another portal. This time I found myself lying on my back in an old hut somewhere deep in a forest. There was an old woman, her back to me, tending a fire and a boiling pot of herbs. As she sang her voice wove with the voice of the ayahuasquero back in the jungle, but before my mind could grasp onto this, my attention was brought to my body. My bones were aching and my muscles were contracting. The old woman sang in a combination of Spanish and some other language, her words magically translated to me. Ayahuasca Medico, "Open her body. Open her spirit. Cleanse, cleanse her body. Bring her back to you Mother." The melody of the song moved over me and through me. My skin lost its elasticity and began to shrivel like an old apple. One by one, the toned and full musculature of my young body turned to energy and slid off my bones and into the earth. My lungs tightened and I gasped for air. The old woman kept singing. Then my bones disintegrated and turned to sand. I could no longer see or feel my physical body.

I heard the woman's voice say, "Fluid awareness. Let your awareness become fluid." Swish, swash went the rhythm of the night. Swish, swash, went the river. Then a man appeared and blew smoke over me. The fire was warm and the wild dance of flames drew me into its yellow, orange core. I became one with the fire as I stared into it. Lighting up the night sky with flames, a voice roared out into the night. Roaring like thunder and pacing the edge of the cliff, back and forth I paced. And then I leapt. Landing with grace at the edge of my parent's bed in the house I grew up in. They were sleeping. "Fluid awareness. Remain in fluid awareness," I heard the voice say again. I climbed off the bed and watched with joyful tears, as memories of my childhood, camping, fishing, family excursions, and all the ways my parents had supported me played out before me. Fading in the back ground, as all these scenes rolled through, my mother and father grew older in years, their bodies died. A bright Light appeared over the remains of their form, leaving me with only the memories and an overwhelming appreciation and love for them. Again, the voice roared out like thunder and I found myself leaping back to the fire and listening to the sound of the jungle and melodic rattle of the shaman. Hands now open at my side and aware of my body a question formed in my mind. "I have experienced my body dying and dissolving into the earth. I've watched flowers and trees grown from seed, blossom and then wither and die and I have seen my parents dissolve before my very eyes. If all this is temporary, then what is real? What is the point?"

At that moment the ayahuasquero changed the rhythm of his rattling and walked toward me. As he approached, I could feel and see my body, not as a bones, muscles and organs, but as pure energy, an exquisite design of rivers of light and color. The tendrils of my energy weaving with the energy patterns of the jungle surrounding me. A path was formed. I let my consciousness merge with the path and as I did, a sweet melody of peace flowed from the lips of the ayahuasquero. The icaro ran through me like warm honey, and vibrational patterns that slowly and gently teased my energy field into the light spectrum of a rainbow. I was no longer in form. I became a fluid river of vibration and color that painted the desert floor with flowers, cacti and lizards. I became one with the ocean and swam with whales, as one of them. Pink and purple sunrises birthed from my heart. Orange-red sunsets swallowed me whole, and flowers bloomed as I walked endless paths of mountains and valleys. I watched and became one with life as its many manifestations bloomed, withered and then died. Over and over, this went on for a while. I was in a state of love with it all. In a state of bliss. And then all at once everything stopped. Silence hung in the air. Nothingness. Just dark and quiet.

Again, the question rose from deep within. "What is the

point? What is the meaning of all of this?" I waited and waited, for what seemed a very long time. I did not understand what was happening. Finally, there was a small pin light in the dark. Watching with full attention as the outline of a circle was drawn in the black sky, the song of the ayahuasquero came back into my awareness. A kaleidoscope of colors poured forth from the blackness forming the answer to my question, as the living energy wove the web of truth for me to witness. Blissful waves of liquid light poured from the heavens and washed through my body, as the first letter of the word formed in a brilliant and luminescent symphony. L appeared in all the colors of the rainbow. Then came O. "No, it can't be," I thought. "Is this really happening?" V was formed and my heart leapt with joy. E was slow to arrive, as though the heavens were playing with me, and then all of a sudden, without realizing how I did it, I was on my feet, dancing to the music of Truth. LOVE. Love is the point and the meaning. Love is the Absolute, the highest expression of the Divine.

Rolling over on my side, I slowly opened my eyes. The ayahuasquero was smiling and smoking his tobacco. Puffs of smoke moved in circles around me. The beauty of the moment was indescribable. Oceans of gratitude washed through every cell and fiber of my being. The gift of that ceremony forever changed my life, my awareness, and my understanding of Munay. May Love be a guiding force, your inspiration, motivation, your companion and your destiny.

Are you ready to move out of fear, out of illusion and into Truth, into the freedom of living in munay?

"The spiritual warrior realizes that the world is her mirror. She understands that to bring change to the world she must first change herself. She knows her battles are within, not with the outer world. The great work of the spiritual warrior is the inner work of self-realization." Chandra Sun Eagle

Cheka

Cheka (check - ah) is the ability to distinguish between relative truths and that of Absolute Truth. As a guiding principle, Cheka challenges us to truly "know thyself". To truly know oneself, we must understand the foundation and premise of our lives, the guiding beliefs and mythologies that have created the framework of our existence. Cheka establishes that there is a myriad of relative truths within the realms of consciousness. There is a governing body of Cosmic Spiritual Law and there is one Absolute Truth of the highest order. That is the truth of Munay - the unconditional, impersonal frequency and force of Love that weaves together all life. Imperative to ascending to the top of Mount Munay, is the work of tracking, uncovering and understanding, in totality, where our personal truths originate from, as well as the source of the relative truths that form the collective consciousness and consensual reality. Through recovering our past and inviting it into the present we are able to identify the various levels of our reality, and how and where the threads of our consciousness and Light Body are woven into collective field. Once we have identified a relative truth, and pull it out of the unconscious and into the light, it becomes negotiable. Hence, we can make a conscious choice as to what remains a part of our foundation and what gets mikhuyed, composted or transmuted. We are then able to reorient and recalibrate our awareness and rewire our Luminous Energy Field with the affinity of our essential self, the forces of nature and Sacred Law.

The Andean people are born into the knowing that we come from the Seed of Creation, and our Core Energetic Essence is infused with the creative intelligence and frequencies of Oneness, Sacredness, Beauty and Love. We do not originate from separation, depression, self-loathing or judgement. These beliefs and frequencies were learned or conditioned into us from this lifetime and previous life times. Countless experiences that have been etched into Luminous Energy Field are afflicting the soul, mind and body of so many in the western world.

As I talked about earlier, when traumatic experiences remain unhealed or unconscious, by default, our past is our present and it becomes our future as well. Why? Because these events have made energetic imprints that have crystalized within the blueprint of our, emotional body and energy body. The imprints are then stored as energy, forming resonance receptors that sit on the edge of the energy body. As electromagnetic beings, we walk around like magnets, drawing to us the circumstances, people and events similar to that of the past, until we reprogram ourselves. The unhealed events and experiences of the past color our perception, formulate the filters through which we "see" the world, and how our reality is crafted. It is the relative truths that have been acquired through en-cultured beliefs and the judgments of individuals, societies and religions that have formed the majority of the collective consciousness and have created the current condition on Earth. This is what we are awakening from. Humanity has been in a slumber, under trance in certain ways, and fortunately at this time many are being activated by the incoming waves of light, pushed toward a higher destiny and to walk a spiritual path.

From the time we are in the womb and through the early stages of childhood, we are learning and developing through the natural act of absorbing everything in our environment. Our conditioning is based in the familial, ancestral, cultural, educational and environmental atmosphere that we grew up in. By the time we are seven years old, all of this programming has rooted itself in neural pathways of our brain and has taken up residence in the subconscious and in the body. If the conditions of our environment stay the same throughout the next 7 to 10 years, our neural network and subconscious mind becomes hardwired with the resulting repetitive messages, beliefs, survival and coping mechanisms. These dominate messages and complexes and then become mindsets, attitudes and crystallized images of who we think we are. Our self-image and beliefs about the world have formed, becoming the causative agents that set off a specific reaction, in any given moment or life circumstance. So when we truly contemplate, and do the work inner work of Cheka, with an open mind, we are opening the doors to "seeing" how much of what we create in our life is a re-creation of past events, emotional wounding, relative truths, and the actual false-truths that have become the dominant creative forces in our individual and collect reality. Many people go through life unaware of all of this, under a kind of hypnotic trance and hypnotic thinking formed during the early years of life. Never realizing that there might be other, more life affirming, spiritually based positive truths, to be operating with. As a collective, we have inherited a memory of struggle and of war from our ancestors, which has overshadowed the light of human potential. However, we don't have to settle for what was, or for how things are. That is a very outdated way of thinking. Shamans understand that just because we were born into a certain of circumstances and with a particular genetic makeup, doesn't mean we can't change it in the present. The mystics of the Andes maintain that we can shift our existence from the realities of our past, and learn to reside in our trans-temporal, eternal nature, while in the body. Through ancient and modern modalities combined, we can transform, and learn sustainable practices of how to source from the unified field of primordial energy, rather than the literal energy of inherited programming. We can become masterful creators, while sourcing Divine energy and the Absolute.

Lifting the veils

Human beings always respond, act, feel and perform in accordance with their self-image, what they believe to be true about themselves, and their surrounding environment. The brain and nervous system are engineered to respond automatically and appropriately to the challenges and problems in our environments. This is how we are built. It is a fundamental law of the mind. Your nervous system cannot differentiate between an imagined state and a real state; therefore your nervous system reacts to what you think is true, imagines taken to be true or what your genetic imprinting tells you is true. Based on this fundamental law, we can see how when the image, the ideas of self or others or our environment are hardwired a specific way, our reaction to the present day or current situation could be inaccurate or inappropriate. And much to the contrary of common belief, we act or fail to act, not because of will or lack of will, but rather because of the hardwiring in our neural pathways and memories held in the subconscious. Imagined truths of who we are, who we are not, what we are capable of, what we are not capable or worthy of, is an exploration that leads to the dissolving of old patterning and the possibility to move our life's direction from one of fate, to one of destiny.

Recently, there have been some very interesting finds in this area of biological science. Epigenetics is the biological study of genetic inheritance and the mechanisms that control gene activity, and how these factors influence the development of an organism. Studies are showing that our genes are encrypted with experiences that not only our mothers and fathers have had, but also their mothers and fathers, and so on down the line. We literally are carrying the imprints and memories of ancestors, that perhaps, we have never even met. The good news is that we can reverse and change how our genetics express themselves.

Working with the law of Cheka is to challenge our internal constructs and what we believe to be true. For a lot of people this is a very difficult thing to do. The level of resistance I witness when working with people, regardless of their desire to heal, can be very frustrating for them, as the calcified patterns often seem insurmountable. Resistance really is just form not wanting to change, so the work takes on a quality of perseverance and will power to compassionately explore these areas of resistance. In other cases, I witness, what I refer to as the magic pill solution. People who want the change without really doing the work, or don't want to give up the old habitual ways. They want to stay in their comfort zone. Well, it doesn't work that way. And right now, we are all being pushed to the max to re-define ourselves, to recalibrate our consciousness, our lives and the world around us, to higher octave of existence.

The second aspect to the path of Cheka is to become fully available to Spirit and to your destiny. Cheka is also a guiding principle when coming to the crossroad. The crossroad where we choose to merge our conscious self (ego sense of personality) with the "High Self". The merging of our self-will with Divine Will. Daily attunement to the High Self and learning to listen to its guidance is our direct path to merging our conscious will with that of Creators will, and developing our Spiritual consciousness. There is a part of us that has not descended into physical matter. That part of us is The High Self, our Essential Being that resides in the luminous realms of our energetic architecture. It is the aspect of our soul that contains the Divine Spark and is in perfect harmony and connection with Creator, but has not descended into physical matter. Our High Self is our guardian angel that looks over us, is all loving and compassionate. It contains all the knowledge and all the power we need to direct our lives in the highest way. Learning to quiet our outer senses and tame the mind takes practice and daily meditation. Not succumbing to distractions of the outside world, or internal world for that matter, and entering the stillness is the only way we will hear the voice of our High Self. Attuning with our High Self awakens the centers of the higher mind and expands our perception to meet that of Spirits voice. But we have to invite and give permission to the High Self and to Spirit, to speak to us and to intervene on behalf of our highest good. We all have free will and this includes the free will to align or not align with our High Self and to follow its guidance.

The mind and consciousness are at the center of philosophical discussions and all mystical traditions. I'd like to share what one of my beloved teachers shared with me in simple terms to help me understand. She said, "It's almost like we have two minds, the personal mind and the higher mind. The mind can be thought of as awareness and is the vehicle for consciousness. The ego mind or personal mind is rational, subjective, filled with filters of personal preferences, constructs and beliefs, etc. The mind doesn't begin or end in the head. In fact, the mind or mental realm is carried in a layer of the energy body. The subconscious aspect of the mind is located based on where it fits with a body part, chakra or gland. As spoken about in the chapter on kausay, imprints and memories left by our ancestors, past lives and childhood conditioning embed themselves in a particular chakra. The emotions of those events and circumstances also get stored in our musculature, organs, skeletal system, brain and neurological pathways. The Higher Mind is connected with our High Self and gives us access to more elevated, impersonal, truth-based perspectives. The Higher Mind is neutral and detached from emotions and personal gain. Most need training in this area, but when we activate the higher mind, we are able to access higher perceptual vantage points, a more global and even universal view. Changing our behavioral and mind patterns takes a tremendous amount of discipline, attention and introspection. Who ever said it would be easy? For anything worthwhile and of value takes time, discipline and hard work. For most of us, surrendering our will to Creator's will, is a gradual process, in which we find ourselves at the crossroad more than once, with a lot of doing, un-doing, and non-doing in between, before higher states of consciousness take precedence. With the power of our will and the guidance from the High Self, we learn to lessen our grip on illusions and egocentric behaviors, initializing the ways of illumination and love through connection with the sacred. The medicine person understands this process of merging the ego with the High Self, and activating the centers of the Higher Mind, as essential to becoming an open vessel for spirit to not only work through us, but as us. In preparation to become the vessel, the initiations and rites of passage a shaman goes through are multileveled and continue throughout their lives. These initiations provide a rich testing ground for the initiate to see where and how their conditioning is living within them, where there is need or potential for growth and refinement, and how to adjust the perceptions their human existence to unite with their own Divinity and Creator. The harmonization and embodied realization that we are Spiritual Light Beings is what gives the shaman the ability to bring about change in extraordinary ways. Change for themselves, their communities, individuals, the animals, the weather etc....

The Andean approach to Cheka, encountering and harmonizing energy

Unearthing the underlying elements of our personal foundation and dissolving the many layers that have kept us from growing and evolving is a constant practice and discipline. Once you dive deep and become actively engaged with the principle of Cheka you may be surprised at what you find and what you encounter. A majority of people are living in a world of contradiction, while attempting to convince themselves that everything is fine. The danger of this, is a developing pattern of disassociating or cognitive dissonance, that leads to further separation from Self. As a whole, during these current times, humanity is fragmented, and under the spell of separation. Many have lost touch with what brings meaning and what is truly important. Without meaning and connection there is despair and depression. Paramount during this phase of collective purification is to not fall into distress or to lose faith. Remember, the new energy has arrived. The Beauty Way, unity, justice and peace will prevail if we all do our inner work. Life will find its way and harmonious flow. It always has and always does. During this passage, and as we each shift our awareness to acknowledging how our relative truths, beliefs, mindsets and attitudes have contributed to the world, challenges and sometimes adversarial relationships will arise. View these circumstances as opportunities to ascend into higher states of consciousness. Don't feed the negativity. Instead, look at the lessons being presented, learn from then and redirect your attention to how you can create more beauty and abundance in your life and for those around you. Shifting your mindset in this manner, immediately shifts your attitude and your perception toward expansion and unity, and allows divine intelligence and truth to anchor through you.

To work more efficiently with this part of our transformation the energetic teachings in the Andean tradition known as tinkuy(teen-qui), tupay (too-pie) and taqe (ta - kay) offer us invaluable teachings and practices.

When faced with adversity or confrontation, the Andean people have a much different approach than we tend to have in western culture. Their approach to navigating the many levels of consciousness and relationships involves a three stage process. This process is enveloped by an understanding that cooperation, not competition, is the way to reach higher ground and create beauty with all physical and spiritual encounters in life.

Tinkuy refers primarily to first stage of encounter, when the energy of two beings, or two animals or two cultures meet for the first time. Tupay is the second stage of the encounter, which involves looking at the various dynamics and energy between the two entities, while determining the best approach; to either diffuse the energy, engage with it or not engage, and walk away. This shift in perception through luminous awareness allows us to come face to face with confrontation and to choose the best approach. The third stage is known as taqe, an exercise of Love, by which the energies are harmonized, joined and woven together.

When applying these principles to our inner work, tinkuy is when circumstances in our life have activated an energetic response and specific reaction from us and we become acutely aware of the triggered or activated energy. Tinkuy is being aware of our fear responses, knee jerk reactions, our copying mechanisms and survival mechanisms, and then confronting ourselves, not avoiding, pushing the situation aside, or blaming the outside world. Tinkuy is the encounter, it is recognizing the meeting of energies as an opportunity to explore and understand the aspects of our past and personal conditioning that have caused the specific reaction.

Tupay, the second stage of the energetic process, involves going deeper into ourselves, our memories, our conditioning and taking inventory of our inner workings. Tupay is the essential place of taking responsibility, not a position. This can a take a considerable amount of time and should not be rushed or brushed over. Depending on the complexity of the imprint you may need outside assistance, such as a shamanic journey to help identify ancestral programming our past life imprints. But you can always begin by going into your childhood of this current life to see how your past has affected you, and how it lives within you, on an emotional, mental and spiritual level. Your main clues are the themes that keep showing up in your adult life.

The third stage of the process, taqe, is about harmonizing the energies within and moving your relationship to Self to higher ground. Healing the wounds, forgiving yourself and others, while celebrating the opportunity to transform, and then blessing the events and people involved with Light. Always encircle the situation and all discordant energies with peace and the Loving presence of your High Self and Creator. Create unity within, let go of being right and all will resolve itself in manner that is in highest for all involved.

Shifting perspective around negative energy, situations and dark forces

When a so-called negative situation arises or comes forward in your life, and it disturbs the balance of your life, you must start working it to lighten your karmic burden and increase your consciousness. Opposing forces and interferences are to be seen as catalysts. Whether you feel you are a victim, or actually have been a victim of an outside circumstance, the truth is that it is now a part of your life, and it is the way in which you respond to the circumstances that determine its effect on you. Responsibility viewed as response-ability, is your ability to respond, not blaming or defaulting to victim consciousness. Working the situation now present in your life is not always pleasant and can be extremely tiring, but it is a good opportunity for growth and should be approached with responsibility. The more you "work" the situation, to the last detail, and keep placing the circumstance is Truth Light, the more Light you will put on yourself and draw toward you. At a certain point, an interesting thing begins to happen. Even where strong curses, spells or psychic attacks were involved, that warped your reality, the more you keep working it to the nth, nth detail, reality shifts to such an extent, that it could appear that the dark, negative force or situation, has done you a great service. Why? Because what started out as very dark, attempting to delay or derail your evolution, after being worked on by the frequencies of Light and Munay, over and over again, the result is that your life and prosperity have jumped ahead several orders of magnitude. You have worked the circumstances of your inner world into such good place that you realize, had you not had the opposing and challenging energies to force you to work harder, and had you been working on our own, using spiritual methods, such as being kind and generous to others, it could have taken twenty years to reach this place you are now. Really sit with this. It's a nugget of gold. Also, remember that in the Andean tradition they don't view energy through the lens of duality, rather through the lens of vibratory resonance. There is hucha, heavy energy and sami, refined, high frequency energy, and the more sami that is present the less hucha we accumulate, and the quicker it is transmuted.

To me this is powerful example of how the Andean people embody the above. The Spanish invaded the native land and Andean culture, destroyed massive amounts of sacred structures, and overlaid their Christian Religion, to the point of building churches on top of some the most powerful energetic centers already established as temples by the Natives. In the past 17 years of traveling in Peru I have not come across one Andean Native who holds resentment or anger about this time or feel contempt for those who adopted the Christian ways. Not to say some don't, but the Andean people and Paqos I know, view that time in history through the eye of the heart - through Munay - and have embraced the Christ Energy as part of their culture as opposed trying to banish it.

A New Myth to Embody

In the late 90's my life began to take on a distinct and lucid quality, as I underwent the beginning stages of initiation, a remembrance, and preparation for this path. A sequence of events rolled through my life that began to shatter how

I saw myself, what I thought was real, and how I viewed the world. This is the moment of my life that I would say when my world began to really turn over. It was the beginning of truly seeing where my energy was locked in an old version of myself, and bound by past conditioning. I was presented daily with the limiting beliefs, and cultural conditioning that was not in alliance with what had been shown to me in following the journey. The spirit world was breaking through and making its way into my life with unrelenting determination.

"Please come in. Make yourself comfortable."

I raised my eyes from the floor to meet the invitation and stepped through the narrow doorway, as the native woman pulled back the grey blanket that covered its opening. I entered a small room that was dimly lit with candles. Shapes and shadows flickered on the walls. Smoke from the burning incense, sage, copal and frankincense, hung in the air. Once my eyes adjusted, I was able to make out some of the objects in the room. I looked around slowly, trying to conceal my nervousness and quiet the chatter inside my head. Feathers, drums, stones, crystals and ancient artifacts adorned the room. A picture of an eagle in flight was to my right, a buffalo standing in a grassy meadow in front of me, and a black bear sauntering through a pine tree forest to my left. All of them possessed life like qualities with the potential to jump out of their frames at any moment. I was not able to identify what was under my feet, but it was definitely some kind of animal pelt. The woman standing before me wore a long sleeve suede shirt with an eagle embroidered on the back. Her hair was dark brown and her skin seemed to match almost perfectly. She had soft, emerald green eyes. The kind that draw you in, leaving you feeling like you've just been on a journey to some unknown, mystical place. I couldn't tell how old she was, but I got the sense she had no age.

A few weeks prior I was talking to friend about a melancholy I had come to realize had been with me most of life. It had recently resurfaced and I'd been trying to get to the root, but I just couldn't. No matter what I tried, meditation, yoga, counseling, there was something hidden from me, and the one word that described the feeling was "longing". As I spoke to my friend, with a loving smile she said, "Chandra, I've been telling you for months about this shaman who I know you need to see. She lives in the mountains outside of Santa Barbara. Here's her number. Call!"

The poised and calm woman before me was patient as I took in my surroundings, until once again my eyes met hers. Still standing, she motioned for me to have a seat on the floor across from her. Her stature was one of strength and grace. Her movements were fluid and mesmerizing. She slowly lowered herself to the floor in front of me. We spoke briefly about why I had come, and then with a slight gesture, she instructed me to lower my chin to my chest. She did the same and then closed her eyes. I closed mine too.

"Follow your breath for a few minutes and when you feel ready match your rhythm to mine." Her voice was warm and assuring and it didn't take long for my breath to match hers. I felt a deep surrender. She seemed to sense this immediately and instructed me to lie down.

"I'm going to journey for you," she said softly, "tracking your soul's path and looking for what will bring healing for you. All you need to do is focus on your breath and relax. When I am finished, we will talk more."

The room was silent for a few minutes and then she began to sing a chant of the Chumash Indians who used to live on the land where I was now lying. The sounds felt familiar and my eyes welled with tears, as the deep boom from her drum held the rhythm of a heartbeat. My breath sped up and then slowed again as the beat of the drum changed to a rapid melodic beat that carried me into other realms and ancient memories.

I felt someone above me, blowing into my chest and running

feathers over my body. Curious, I opened my eyes, but no one was there and the shaman was still at my feet drumming. There was no time for trying to make sense of this, because almost as quickly as I had opened my eyes, they fell shut with heaviness and I was out again. This happened a few more times throughout the drumming, until slowly the beat changed back to gagong, gagong, pause, gagong, gagong, and she began to chant that beautiful song she began the journey with. This time it brought a smile to my face. The singing stopped and there was a long pause of silence as I regained "my senses". Like a child, I felt excited to share all that I saw during the journey, but she shushed me gently and began to speak. "Leave your eyes closed and listen. Listen intently." Her voice was still soft, but firmer now, as to stress the importance of what I was about to hear. "The journey was good and we brought back much for you. A long time ago you lived as I and many other medicine people live today, close to the earth and practicing ancient ways of healing. Your soul longs to return to this and it is time. Many other souls will be awakening to the call and remembering the old ways. You have a strong connection with the Mother Earth and part of the sadness you feel is her pain. As humanity continues to stray from living in harmony with her and each other, you feel this pain as well. You must spend more time sitting and walking in nature, moving slowly, observing the animals and the elements. Pay close attention to your dreams. They will guide you, giving you important messages and clues along the way. You will be guided to other lands and traditions. Teachers will come, bringing gifts and teachings for your journey, but remember that the true teacher is within. I have retrieved aspects of your soul. These seeds of your soul and their qualities will develop over time as you nurture them. Your destiny is in your hands and it is your choice what you do with it. I have spoken the words of the ancestors and so it is." She then lifted herself from the floor and helped me to my feet, holding my ankles and encouraging me to breathe deeply into her hands. "Can I see you again?" I asked. Her answer was confusing to me, but it was obvious.

"You have what you need to go forward. Go knowing that you do not walk alone." She gave me a long hug and placed a stone in my hand. "Carry this with you." And then she guided me to the small opening where I had first entered the room. I walked down the rock path that led to my truck, noticing that the sadness I came with had lifted. I wanted desperately to remember everything that had happened and everything she had told me. My body felt light and unencumbered, like I could walk and walk and never get tired. "Maybe I could walk home," I thought. But the home I felt like walking to seemed oceans and lands away.

After my session with the Chumash Medicine Woman I continued studying various modalities of bodywork, Polarity Therapy, and cranial sacral unwinding. Understanding the source of my melancholy eased it tremendously, as the visions and messages from that journey constantly whispered in my ears.

I did still find myself encumbered with a belief that it wasn't possible for me to be who she said I was, mainly because I had not grown up in the traditional ways, and had no mother or grandmother to teach me the ancient wisdom ways. I had to learn how to match the strength of that limiting belief. I turned my stubbornness into my ally. I was determined. I kept working the process. My living prayer became stronger and stronger with time. Fortunately, the force of my will and the force of Spirit, outweighed the doubt that arose from the belief. The stronger I prayed, the stronger the spirit world shook and answered back. It shook with such intensity, imbuing my reality with undeniable and constant messages of who I am and what I was here to do. Lifelike dreams of other times, other worlds, initiations and rites of passage were a nightly occurrence. I would often wake up, disoriented, not knowing where I was. Worlds and realms were colliding and coalescing within me. The dreams came in sequences and left puzzling messages for me to decode. Vivid, distinct, visceral dreams, one right after the other, along with literal visitations from Spirit guides in the night, marked the significant passage of the death and rebirth I was going through. It is what is known as the classic shamanic awakening. My first totem animal came in the dreamtime, and the next day, while in the mountains, we met each other in physical presence. The currents of resolve flowed. I was saying yes, with all I had. And Spirit was matching my commitment and willingness. As I untethered my soul from the relative truths that were no longer truths for me my entire world shifted on its axis.

Whirling Rainbow Prophecy

In the Hopi and Navajo tradition there is a prophecy known as the Whirling Rainbow of Peace. This prophecy denotes a time when children with light eyes, who speak of love as the healer of all children and life on the earth, will seek out the wisdom of the Indigenous Elders. They are known as the Children of Rainbow, who have white skin and will pursue new ways of understanding themselves and the world, that are not taught in the western world. To the Hopi and Navajo these children signify that the Ancestors have come back in white bodies, but are red on the inside. These children of the Rainbow will learn to walk the Mother Earth in balance and will assist in changing the consciousness and ways of the white chiefs. Coming from all four corners of the Earth, the warriors of the rainbow, will come with an understanding that there is no superior race, and that all colors and creeds are equal. All pathways to wholeness are to be respected and they are to work together in unity. These warriors will be tested along the way and their ability to stay on the scared path. Many will succumb to delusion and lower vibrational tendencies, others will get lost, but will eventually find their way back, while others will preserver and experience a quickening and remembering. Colorful dreams will be brought to these warriors in the Dreamtime, reminding them of who they are and how to walk the Sacred Path, bringing balance and peace to the Earth Mother and humanity.

The Shaman's way of shifting their reality

This process of identifying and navigating our relative truths is a process of not only becoming aware of the stories that have colored our reality, but for the shaman, paqo or medicine person, this is a process that takes place on energetic level, in congruence with the three levels of reality and three fundamentals levels of consciousness. It is not solely an exercise of the mind and clearing of emotions through psychotherapy that the western world is accustomed to. It is a full transformation at all levels of their being and all levels of reality.

In light of your "becoming" I invite you to discover the root of the relative truths of your story and the consensual truths of society that have been informing your reality. Free your energy identifying habitual patterns, so that your soul can find its way. The great transition that we are all going through is a period of purification, in which, we and the Pacha Mama are shedding and shaking off the imprints of dense, outworn and outdate templates. We are ascending into a higher vibration and the higher light of creation. As we ascend in consciousness and waves of cosmic frequencies enter our atmosphere, our abilities and power will increase. Hence, it is necessary to clear the egoic tendencies, so that our ego does not become more boisterous or delusional. It is important to develop discernment and know if you are acting with humility and gratitude, or if the ego has become inflated, and you are acting from a place of righteousness or judgment. Understanding that nothing is created in our outer world that isn't a reflection of our inner world, and thus we have the power to dissolve and deconstruct the manifestations that were created from ignorance or fear. We have the power to rebuild our world in communion with our Heart's and the Heart of Creator. Respect for the free will of all is to be honored. Cultivate true happiness or peace within. Stop looking to the outside world for validation or stability. Play in the wheel of life, show up fully in world, but do not get so attached to outside experiences and events that they become the breaking point of your inner peace.

Key elements to working with Cheka

We are intrinsically connected to the spiral of evolution, the Earth and the transformation she is going through. The Earth is moving into a higher octave of frequency. We live not only on her belly, but as a part of her. She is our Mother. If we resist our own upper movement in consciousness, we become misaligned with what is happening on a cosmic level. We'll become split in our energy, and feel dis-connected with our Mother Earth. We might feel lost or ungrounded, as the old paradigms of our world continue to shatter and during this phase of purification. As Earth moves into the next level of her vibration, it may seem as though time is speeding up. Stay grounded. Slow down. Be present. Stay disciplined with your inner work. As we go through this phase of deconstruction, more and more events are happening in a shorter amount of time, creating more feelings and stronger emotional reactions. This is our opportunity to accelerate our own growth. It is our opportunity to see how our perceptions and relative truths create our world. The masters and mystics of the Andes have been trying to get us to understand that our reaction and experience of an event is based on our interpretation, our own projection and creation of it. And until we realize and take responsibility for our part, whatever the ultimate truth and solution is, it will elude us.

A good way to monitor your progress, as you begin to move

upward through the spiral of ascension is to look at the quality of your relationships to the Earth and the natural world, to Spirit, to the Elements and to others. Are they harmonious, truthful and meaningful?

In ancient times, before one would be admitted into the Mystery Schools, one had to be socially and psychologically balanced. Life itself is our Mystery School today and it provides every experience we will ever need to learn the lessons we need to evolve, to align with our destiny and raise our frequency, to activate our inner sun, and to develop clarity and stability in all areas of your life. Remember that we are coming to the close of an age, and moving into a new cycle. A time of beauty, in which we will all awaken to and encounter the spiritual nature of all life.

Also, remember that embarking on the task of recovering and healing the past is everyone's responsibility. Your ego may not want to. Your fear of the unknown and your attachments to beliefs, the familiar, and the material world may not want to die, but it is time. It is a death everyone must go through to unite with the divine within. And it is the only way our collective soul will find the freedom it seeks. When we recover and heal our past, we free ourselves from the chains that bind us to the unconscious. We become equipped to practice presence and live in the heart's desire. How much of your life is held in the past by unresolved issues, anger or resentment? How much of your life is spent worrying about the future or clinging to material objects in search of security?

As stated above, essential to conscious, spiritual evolution is self-monitoring. Watching the Self in every moment. It is also important to commit to a teacher and to a spiritual path. Being on a spiritual journey and being on a spiritual path are different. I have heard time and time again from people that they don't want to give their power to a teacher. That they are their own teacher and guru and this is what they want to awaken to. Well, the fact of the matter is, that in the beginning of our journey to healing and awakening, we all have blind spots, areas of denial and ingrained patterns that prevent us from seeing ourselves clearly. And therefore we need a spiritual teacher and guide, someone who has walked and encountered the many stages, and various trappings and pitfalls along the way, who can see truth, and has the skills to assist. A true teacher or guide will always help you get in touch and listen to your inner wisdom. A true teacher of integrity will never need to hook into your energy and will always assist you to empower yourself. They can see where you are and will know the appropriate methods to use, tools and teachings to impart at the appropriate time that are specific to your needs. To think that we don't need someone outside of us is, in my opinion is a bit delusional and egocentric. When you commit to a spiritual path and a teacher, that teacher is in turn committing themselves to you and your highest good. The agreement goes both ways. It is the teacher's responsibility to allow Spirit to direct, to listen and to know what leverage to apply and when. It is student's responsibility to live the teachings to the best of their ability, while being their authentic self. It's guaranteed to be challenging. But committing and staying the course, will take the confusion out of your life. You'll begin to see yourself with more clarity. You'll come to know with such intimacy, your strengths and your weaknesses. You'll learn what you are capable of what and not. You'll become more centered. Self-realization leads to God realization. To know thyself is the path to knowing God. Work with where you're at, diligently. Don't compare yourself to others. Drop the competition. Work with what comes up from inside. Breathe into your inner world, and track the origins of arises. It's all right there. When you find an opposing belief, construct or mythology, bring it to your conscious awareness through contemplation, looking back through your life. This conscious act will bring light to the recesses of your psyche and will set in motion the release and transmutation process of the unconscious. More energy gets freed up, more self-empowerment develops and confusion gets cleaned out. Knee jerk reactions turn to appropriate responses. Discipline is key. Relative truths and dominant lies, that have been crafting our reality, are seen for what they are and loosen their grip on us, as we begin to discern the difference between relative truth and Absolute Truth. Becoming aware of these aspects of consciousness, we are taking the first step towards self-empowerment, healing and communing with the Absolute. As we go through our process of disillusionment and clearing of social conditioning, we start to realize that most of what we have associated with is not based in truth or authenticity. As we confront the lies we've been telling ourselves, truth within and without starts to reveal itself. The more we uncover our shadow aspects, wounds and traumas within, the more we can see it in others. We start to see the unseen, the reality of energy exchanges happening between people. Everything we have been hiding and suppressing starts to come to the surface. Darkness within and without starts to be made conscious, and from the dark we emerge into Light. We all have the opportunity to dream and create a new story, one in alignment with our destiny, not our fate.

I have come to understand a large aspect of Cheka, as a process of "dissolving the layers of time." Dissolving the layers of life times of accumulation, contracts and karmic agreements that had run their course and needed clearing. Peeling away all the layers that no longer serve my Being or align with my divinity and connection to Spirit. The treasures I've discovered and continue to discover have re-activated extraordinary potentials I had mastered in other lifetimes, and now I am re-instating these gifts. I can now see where the consensual truths that create feelings and beliefs that we are separate from God and separate from nature originate. I see how asleep most people are. Waking has been both joyous and painful. That's the nature of the path. We have to make our own pilgrimage to the top of Mount Munay. We can walk, we can run, we can make it easy or hard, but it is a climb of endurance and reward beyond your wildest imaginings. Recover your serpent essence and shed the past. Recover your Puma essence and walk with courage. Recover your Condor/Eagle essence and soar into clarity and freedom.

*"The higher we want to rise, the deeper we must go. Ascension is
a process of ascending and descending at the same time. With each
evolutionary cycle we are drawn a little closer to the center where
Heaven and Earth meet." Chandra Sun Eagle*

Kollary

The spiritual law of Kollary (coy-yari), provides a map to full
soul embodiment. Our ability to flow and change, while shifting
our relationship to time, from one of linearity, to the eternal
nature and fluid structure of time and space, are the teachings
of Kollary, which establishes that the fundamental experience
of creation is FLUID. Where there is life there is movement.
It is a prime directive in the Universe. We live in an electrical
universe, where everything vibrates with an energetic frequency
and everything is in a continual state of motion. Nothing is
ever perfectly still and nothing rests. At the most fundamental
level, the Universe and everything which comprises it, is
pure vibratory energy manifesting in a multitude of ways.
The Universe has no solidity as such. Matter is merely energy
configurations in a state of vibration based on the consciousness
directing and informing its structure.

Kollary guides us to the understanding of how to bring the
formless into form, and when it is time, how to release the form
back into the spiral of life for transmutation, to be re-vibrated
and reconfigured. Life is constantly changing, and in order to
come into our fullest, truest nature, to fully participate in life,
we too, must be in flow with the dynamic interaction of the
Universe, and the endless flow of creation.

How do we, on an individual level, allow ourselves to
change, to let go, and embrace a new expression of self? From
the shamanic perspective, as well the quantum perspective,
our degree and level of connectivity to our true nature and the

world around us, is in direct relation and proportion to our state of fluidity. With this realization the Paqo understands and accepts that she wakes each day with the knowing that she is not the same person she was yesterday. And yet, she is still connected with her essential nature, that aspect of her that has no beginning, has no end, and is changeless. She remains aware of her eternal, immortal aspect of her Highest Nature. In the words of Thoth, the Atlantean, from the Emerald Tablet Transcripts, "Ye must become formless in order to become One with the Light."

Kollary is also about fully understanding how one participates with Life, one's availability to the journey and the mapping of one's reality in congruence with the forces of the cosmos. It is about awakening so deeply to the sacred evolutionary impulse of the heart of the universe, and weaving our existence with the center of creation, that our life becomes a dance, and an extraordinary expression of the highest potential, a radical and unimaginable unification with the source of our most Divine True Nature.

For the Paqo, everything in the Universe, in the realm of time and space, has a cyclic beginning and end, and it is imperative to recognize and map these shifts, so the journey of life flows and can take its natural course. So that life is more meaningful, fulfilling and participatory. The Andean Paqo's desire and responsibility is to be fully present in the process of life, to practice presence in every moment. What does it really mean to be present? Everything is available to us in the present moment; thus, to be in the here and now is dependent on where our focus is and how much conscious control we have to keep it focused, grounded and centered in the moment. For the Paqo, being fully present in the "process" of life is beyond witnessing, observing or focusing their attention and efforts on personal results. Full presence and participation with life involves a profound level of engagement with creation's ever-changing circumstances, a complete and utter dedication to their "availability" to the journey, and the realization of their true nature, all the while abandoning any and all ego driven modes of operation that may arise. Being present in the process of life rather than in a fixed state of perception, the Paqo is able to see through the expansive spiral nature of time, all streams of fated timelines and all streams of possibility. They are then able to access the most obscure and unique lines of destiny their soul has to offer them. The concept of linear time is expelled, sacred time is entered and altering the course of one's life and the collective journey of humanity becomes a reality.

To truly "know" Thyself, we have to live, we have to experience and offer ourselves fully to Life. We will never get there by reading about how others got there, or by watching from the safety of life's shores. We must find the courage to jump into the river and allow the currents of life and the Great Mystery to carry us back home. I recall a very powerful night in the high Andes. It was during my first sacred pilgrimage back to a familiar land that my soul knew well, when a cosmic gateway of Light opened and invited me to step through and into a bigger river.

Salkantay

As I looked around the candle lit tent, smoke from the burning herbs and incense filled the small space. My body ached from several, long days of hiking and sleeping on the hard ground in high altitude. I had been also experiencing the hours of the night, that were supposed to be filled with rest and sleep, were the best hours for the spirits, of whom I have come to know as "my team," to pay their visits, to make their introduction and to impart messages. Sleep had been virtually impossible the two weeks prior, but my energy was high. That evening I sat in a circle with my fellow shamans in training. Pasqal and Francisco, shamans of the Q'ero nation, our guides and teachers for the past week, worked meticulously and prayerfully in creation of the ceremonial Despacho offering for Apu Salkantay. We were a small group of students from different parts of the world. For most, this pilgrimage was a destination after many years of study. The majority of the group had been studying the Andean path for years and were full mesa carriers. I on the other hand had no special cloth, stones or talismans of power. For me the journey came early on my path, after a visitation from the Apu spirit of Salkantay itself came in the night, and sent a cord of light to my heart, asking if I would answer the call of my Sponsor Mountain. I did not know what it meant to have a sponsor mountain, but with great enthusiasm I answered.

After several days of trekking, I now sat in a sacred circle, situated high in Andes, at the base Apu Salkantay, one of the twelve holy mountains that Q'ero shamans' source from. For the Q'ero medicine people the Apus are the earthly homes for the Illuminated ancestors that once walked in the physical, as masters of the Living Energy. Their wisdom teachings and luminous nature can be felt and seen in these high holy places, and it is to the Apus that the initiate of the Andean Spiritual Path must travel. Tonight, was the night we would receive the karpay (kar-pie), energetic transmission of Salkantay. We huddled close to ward off the cold air of 14,000 feet, while Pasqal and Francisco prayed to the Apu for her blessing. Pasqal motioned to Francisco, then turned to Apu Salkantay. He spread his arms and narrowed his eyes. His appearance took on that of a condor, summoning the powers of the Apu into our circle. I watched in awe as the atmosphere in the tent became palpable with magical sounds. Whistles, mysterious voices and colorful lights filled the air and moved around us. It was time. My stomach was in doing flip flops with excitement and my heart pounded inside my chest. Chanting, rattling, blowing into our chakras, running their mesas over our energy bodies, one by one Pasqal and Francisco transmitted the karpay to each of us and welcomed us, as brothers and sisters, into their family. I was overwhelmed by the sincerity, dedication and openness with which the Q'ero Indians embraced each of us. I felt a part of something so big, so ancient and so sacred. Open. Awake. Light headed and full of wonder, after the close of the ceremony I stumbled to my tent and collapsed in a heap. Falling into a deep sleep for the first time in weeks. But, in what felt like only seconds later, I was suddenly awakened with a tremendous pressure in my lungs, in my head, and in my entire body. My breathing was very shallow and the thought crossed my mind, "Is this what death feels like? I must call out to someone." It felt like my body was collapsing in on itself. Attempting to speak, no sound would come out of my mouth, so I slowed my breathing and relaxed into the tightness. It was then that I heard a voice coming from outside myself. I had not heard this voice before. It was a woman's voice telling me to relax and trust. I opened my eyes and could faintly make out the shape of figure with long hair and flowing clothes. Am I dreaming? Is this real? In a soft and reassuring tone, she began to speak of my soul's journey and asked if I was ready to see deeper into the nature of reality. Telepathically she read the curiosity and yes in my mind, and asked, "Well then, are you ready to die?"

"Ready to die? Not sure about that." I answered back without saying anything. "Try to relax," she said. "You are only dying to an old self, an old perception of the world and another level of who you think you are. It's time to walk with courage and reclaim your power as a medicine woman. This is your path and your gifts are needed in the world." My mind was racing.

More sternly now, the woman hovering above me, told me take a deep breath into my heart. As I did, another dimension and layer of vision opened. Descending from the stars above was the largest spider I had ever seen. As Grandmother Spider descended from the Milky Way, opulent filaments of Light streamed behind her, making a circular web of light with an opening in the center. Instantly I was pulled through my heart chakra, and out of my body, through the opening of Grandmother's web of Light. I was outside of time, beyond the confines of the physical world, swimming through an ocean of stars. The Angel Goddess and I were swimming through the Milky Way. Keenly aware of the stars around me I was also aware of my physical body lying in the tent at the base of Salkantay. I took another breath and looked into the eyes of my guardian. Her eyes sparkled with love, transmitting the message of surrender, so I released my hesitation and spread my wings. The beautiful goddess by my side continued with her teachings as we floated, swam and flew through a galaxy of stars and tribes of celestial beings. We met other spirit teachers along the way who lovingly caressed my head and imparted words of wisdom. This is what I remembered in the morning. "It is not an easy path. Along the way you will be tested. This is not your first initiation and there are many more to come. It is important to keep your physical body, and nervous system strong and healthy, so more light can anchor through you Work on clearing the clutter from your mind and continue to notice where you have resistance. Free yourself from what you have accepted as truth, and completely drop the need to fit into the social consensus of reality. There is a greater truth that awaits you. Turn the perception that fear is your enemy into seeing it as an ally. Reestablish trust in your immediate intuition. Remember to laugh and not take yourself too seriously when intensity arises. Engage life in a sacred manner and know in your heart that all life is to be honored and learned from. You will always be guided. Share what you learn along the way, otherwise the wisdom of the exchange will not be completed."

There was a Native Grandfather. The wrinkles on his brown, leathery face were as deep as canyons that had formed over thousands of years. His eyes were inviting and dancing in the green of his iris was The "Great Star Nation". The old man studied me in silence for a long time. I could not see the rest of his body, and he said nothing as my guide in white and I waited patiently. I felt uncomfortable about staring, but couldn't help it as I drifted deeper into the timelessness held within his gaze. The love that enveloped me was almost too much and I found it difficult to receive. His Love had drawn me into a deep and expanded space within infinity when two objects appeared and the ancient voice of this timeless soul began to speak.

"You see two pipes before you. One of them belongs to you. You carried it many lifetimes ago. It has been living with the Star Nation and if you recognize the one that is yours it signifies the time for its return to the earthly plane, and it will come to you in physical form when you are ready. Do you recognize your pipe?"

I had no doubt and pointed to the one that was singing my name.

"That is right. Now continue on your journey." Following those last words, his lips gently pursed together and blew a billowing breath of sacred tobacco smoke over my body. At that point my attention was brought back to the stars as they lit up in sequence to the beat of a drum in the distance and the rhythm of the night. In that moment I understood the meaning of "Oh Great Star Nation, my brothers and sisters" and the eternal connection to the star seeds within. Descending through Grandmother Spider's web I was gently returned to my body that lay shivering in the mountain air and I fell deeply asleep. The next morning, I woke with a vivid sense of expansiveness and an unexplainable knowing of the meaning of Oneness.

Other teachings and events of times to come were revealed to me that night, guidance I was to not speak of. Some I could recall the next morning, and others presented themselves over the following years. I'm sure there is more to be revealed, but the most vivid and essential messages were the state of love and unity I felt that night, as I was shown and reconnected with aspects of my soul that required the courage to say "YES". Yes, to dying to my former self, yes to embracing the unknown of who I was becoming. On our path to full soul embodiment, we will have to choose, again and again. It is always within our free will.

Embodied Freedom

It is the "embodiment" of the processes of creation, and allowing the flowering of creation to happen through us, with no attachment to an end result, that frees our spirit to be one with all, and to be the vessel through which Spirit works. When we are able to approach life in this manner, we create an opportunity to experience life in all of its glory and timeless, unbound nature. Most people in the western world relate to time as linear. The medicine person and indigenous people do not experience time in a linear, cause and effect fashion, that states when this happens, then that happens, and so on, and that's the way life is. We experience it as circular and spiral in nature, with the ability to heal and change how the past lives within us, while simultaneously shifting future possibilities to probabilities. Remember earlier in the chapter on Munay, when speaking of creating and engaging life from the heart, we move into the quantum field where anything is possible. Linear time is how the logical mind makes sense of its surroundings and organizes reality, which in turn cuts us off from a fundamental truth of creation, that everything in the universe is in constant, dynamic movement.

Everything in the Universe, in the realm of time and space, has a cyclic beginning and end. As discussed previously, this percept is known as a pacha (paw-cha) in the Andean tradition. The law of Kollary orients the Paqo toward engaging life in a spiral, non-linear fashion. The continuous opening and closing of cycles are marked as important shifts in the medicine person's life, and it is imperative to track and map these cycles so the journey of life is lived more consciously, with ease and natural flow. Thus, the practice of trust, vision, intent and timelessness are essential to the Paqo. It is their level of preparedness and readiness that allow shamans to engage fully when opportunity intersects life.

The recognition of pachas also creates accordance with nature and the shaman's environment in which they live. There are smaller or shorter pachas and there are bigger or longer pachas. Pachas also refer to the cycles of the moon, the seasons, and our solar systems movement through astrological signs as well as the Earth's movement through the Milky Way. They are all cycles within the grander picture of Cosmic Creation, cycles within cycles.

Don't sit in opposition to flow, in opposition to your destiny. Otherwise the universe will kick you in the butt. Life is always sending us signals and messages. Sometimes those messages are indicating that it is time to let go of something or someone, to move on from a particular belief or pattern or to adopt a new way of organizing our reality. Recognizing the closing of a particular cycle in our life, is to consciously bring completion to unfinished business and to let go of what is not needed or does not serve us in our next stage of evolution. When we don't recognize the signs life is sending or we choose to ignore them, the messages will get louder and more pronounced until we have no choice but to address what is demanding our attention. If we cling to the past, not allowing for endings, and do not bring healing or completion to things of a particular cycle, we drag the accumulated energies into our next phase or pacha. Examples of this are moving from adolescence to adult hood, but refusing to leave childish behaviors behind, or moving out of a relationship, but not forgiving the other and not cutting the cords to the other. If we hang on to anger or resentment, we don't actually complete the pacha. If a person is refusing the nudge of change, the possibility of a dramatic or traumatic, life changing event, that is out of their control, is commonly experienced. We've all heard stories, or perhaps have experienced firsthand, the undergoing of extreme illness or accidents that create a massive crisis in life. The crisis then became the catalyst for great change and awakening. Viewing external, life altering events, like losing a job or getting divorced, as the divine agents of change, that are forcing you out of your comfort zone, is a healthy and expansive perspective to hold. Crisis, from the shamanic perspective, is not a bad thing. It's not always necessary, but when a crisis does happen it is seen as what was needed to push the individual or group of individuals out of the old and into new terrain. We don't have to and shouldn't wait for crisis or something dramatic to happen to start making the changes and working our life. Do it now. Slow Down. Cultivate stillness within while in being in motion. Listen. Meditate. Pay attention. Be diligent. Notice what comes up in response to your life situations. The more you do this the more attuned to the subtle realms of energy and undercurrents within you will become.

The actuality of awakening to this radically different way of being, no matter how intense the desire, is not always easy. Most people hold so much fear inside that their instinct is to want to control, push against, cling to the familiar, or try to maintain composure in an attempt to avoid pain. So much unnecessary resistance and suffering is created and compounded by doing so. Pain is a natural part of human life. Suffering does not have to be. We suffer because we sacrifice the present for the "could have and should haves" of the past, and fear based "what ifs" of the future. The only thing we have some control of is how we chose to accept and respond to life. And even then, there are moments when we lack the knowing of how to respond and contribute to the moment appropriately. It is in these moments that surrendering into our vulnerability of "not knowing," will move us into the sanctuary of our heart. Into realness. For it is through this vulnerability that healing happens and the Light can enter. We like to think we can control things and perhaps this is why man has created an artificial world of hierarchy of power that thrives on ignorance and fear and people controlling other people. There is no one to blame, only new choices to make. The timing and nature of each individual's process with life and with their destiny is different. Allow it to be so, while remaining committed to a higher path and vision of beauty.

There is no formula or one answer that can be given for mastering the art of fluidity, but to be open to the reality that everything is always changing, and therefore so are you, is essential. To be fully participatory with your destiny, your soul journey and your awakening, you must access the part of you that is ready and willing to let go and to flow. This is actually a very exciting principle, because who you are tomorrow may be different than who you are today. At each sunrise we have the chance to choose the new beginning before us. There is an ever-present possibility to experience freedom and liberation in life while living your heart's desire and in a joyful and meaningful manner. No matter how difficult the previous day was, the rising sun offers a new day of opportunity. Perhaps you are already living in this realm of consciousness and the expressions of it will continue to unfold, helping to lift the collective to more elevated states of joy.

Change is the one constant in our world. Nothing remains the same as life is continually moving. Life, Death and Rebirth are natural cycles and are happening all around us and within us all the time. The weather is different each day. The seasons are continually changing. The Earth never stops spinning as it rotates around the sun and the moon rotates around the earth, affecting the oceans tides. Calibrating with the natural and cosmic cycles aligns us with the greater forces of universe. Personally, I love change and tend to thrive on the dynamics of motion. It's hardwired into my core and is intrinsic to my nature.

For me it is easy and essential for my wellbeing. Being in motion feels natural because of my deep connection to the rhythms of the universe and the elements. And I understand change is not so natural or easy for everyone. Resistance to change prevents energy from flowing. Blocked energy that remains stagnant turns toxic and diseased. Sustained periods of resistance will have an effect on all levels of your being, the physical body, the mind and the soul. Life force diminishes and the body's innate healing mechanism is hindered, inspiration tends to wane and the mental constructs and beliefs become more solidified. Practice responding when opportunity intersects with your life. Life is happening and it's going to continue to happen. Be proactive and re-calibrate your internal timing with the sacred timing, celestial movements, and seasonal shifts of the natural order. Learn to engage fully. Cultivate a life that brings qualities of light and love to you and that assist with the flowering of your being and the ever-evolving state of fulfillment, transforming you into your next shape, your next form and Self.

The Collective Flowering

In relation to collective evolution, we, the children of earth, are directly connected to the spiral of evolution, the earth and the transformation she is going through. The Earth is moving into a higher octave of vibration, and we are a part of her. These higher frequencies transfer to the Earth's magnetic grid and then to our energy field and through our consciousness. Our connection to the Earth's resonance provides a continuum of energy exchange. The energy pulsing through Earth's magnetic grid and her ceke system, affects how we feel and think and evolve. Avoiding or resisting change, and your upward movement in consciousness, you risk missing a sacred opportunity to align with your Cosmic Self. As the earth moves into the next level, her vibration lifts, many are experiencing a sense that time is speeding up. And yet, at the center of every person, and the center of every experience there exists quiet, stillness and truth. Nature exemplifies this truth, as at the center of every hurricane, tornado or whirlpool there is absolute calm and peace. And deep within each of us, at our core, that same peace and calm can be found. Learning to quiet the outer senses and go within you will find this point of stillness. As we all go through this collective purification, more and more events are happening in a shorter amount of time, resulting in an intensified time. Opportunity is knocking, encouraging us to see how our perceptions of the past are creating suffering and resistance to evolution.

Voice of the Grandmother

On the Bolivian side of Lake Titicaca, there is a very small island named Isla de la Luna, Island of the Moon. The temple area is at the very top and maintained by the few Aymara women who live on the island. I could feel the exquisitely soft, yet powerful energy of the island emanating out into the waters before the boat reached the shoreline. After cleansing my chakras and energy field with the electrical waters of the Lake, I made my way up the short path to the top. Offering a silent prayer from my heart, and a k'intu (keen -tu) of five coca leaves at the entrance, I then walked the perimeter of the ancient grounds, three times in a counter clockwise direction. With each rotation my body and awareness descended into the Pacha Mama. After completing the third round I felt the pull to walk from where I stood in the East direction, to center, then paused and continued to the West. After a moment of connecting with the energies of the West I turned and walked back to the center, and then to the North, connecting with the Light Beings of the ceremonial altar. I then made my final 180 degree turn and walked to the South and sank into a deeply beautiful meditation. A Grandmother Spirit appeared before me, bringing a message she wanted to be shared. She spoke lovingly, "The great change has already begun. The Feminine principles of creation are rising and being re-birthed. Women of the world, Sisters, it is your innate and inherent connection to the Cosmic Mother and the Mother Earth that is calling you to awaken, to rise, join hands, and give birth to the new life. With fierce love and temperance, awaken the wise and free woman within. Treat your body as a temple. Call to the loving and wise Grandmothers who circle your planet. We are waiting for you to reach out and ask for our help. Light your sacred fires and gather the people to sing, dance and invoke the strength and protection of the Grandfathers. Awaken the Universal Flow of Love held within the womb of creation by awakening to your own self-love. Nurture the seeds of your dreams and the dream of Mother Earth, that all her children will once again walk in beauty upon her belly. Embrace your masculine qualities and celebrate the sacred union within. Rise and embody your fullest potential. The world needs you. Men of the world, brothers, lay to rest your weary ways of the old. There is no need to fear the rising of the feminine. Join her on the altar of love and equanimity. Ignite the Divine spark and wield your sword of reverence, your sword of truth and your sword of protection. Join arms with your brothers through the shield and codes of honor, disseminated by the Lords of Light and the Brotherhood of a Higher Order. Embrace your feminine qualities and celebrate the sacred union within. Rise and meet your highest and fullest potential. The world needs you."

I bowed in reverence to the Grandmother Spirit, as she faded from my vision, sitting for a long time in the wake of her potent words and loving embrace, until it was time to go, carrying with me deep knowing that the unifying force of the Cosmic Mother would prevail.

Our Multi-dimensional Nature

In relation to coming into our fullness, there is an aspect to this that shamans and mystics have mastered through years of spiritual practices and spiritual initiations. What I'm referring to is our multi-dimensional nature and the multi-dimensional nature of reality. To help in our understanding of this, it's important to understand how the ancients of many indigenous cultures view physical reality. In the Andean tradition reality is seen and experienced as multi-layered or multi-tiered. The nature of this physical reality, that we experience with our five senses and inhabit physically, is not limited to a linear time concept or a one-dimensional plane. Rather, the nature of this physical plane, and therefore the nature of humanity, is not limited to what we experience through our five senses, nor are we defined by a one-dimensional plane of existence. There is more to this reality than meets the eye, so to say. It has been, and remains to this day, the shamanic ceremony, shamanic journey, mystical and spiritual training that have prepared the shaman to enter these other realities and realms, in order heal the events of the past and change the possibilities of the future. Linearity does not exist for the shaman or Paqo. They exist in the present, with connection to the cyclic, spiral and multi-dimensional aspect of time. This is where the medicine of hummingbird comes in.

Hummingbird Medicine and the Epic Soul Journey

Long, long ago, when the Children of the Sun needed to send a message to Wiracocha (Creator), they requested the presence of Great Condor. As the largest bird, with the widest wing span and the ability to fly higher than any other bird, the Andean Condor was considered the King of the skies and archetypal force of the Hanaq Pacha or Upper World, and therefore was considered the most likely candidate to be the primary messenger between the people and their Creator in the Heavens. At the command of the Andean High Priest, Condor was about to take flight, when the tiny and colorful spirit of hummingbird appeared and said wait, "I should be the one to carry the messages to Wiracocha and I should be the messenger of the Heavens, for not only can

I fly to edge of the sky, but I can fly beyond the edge and into the very center." All the other birds laughed and the Andean High Priest patted hummingbird on the head, and with a sweet gesture said, "But, little bird, you are too small to make this journey. Your wings will tire before you reach your destination. Let the biggest bird of the sky, the Great Condor do this job." And with that Condor took to the skies, flying past the Sun towards the edge of the sky. Just before reaching exhaustion, Condor reached the edge of the sky. Following the one rule that he was not to look Wiracocha in the eye, he turned his back, extended his wing into the vast heaven and called to Wiracocha. Just as Wiracocha appeared, out from under the giant black and white plumes of Condor's wings came little hummingbird, flying beyond the edge of the sky and into the center of the Upper World, where Wiracocha stood in his heavenly garden. Calling to the little one in a futile attempt to get hummingbird to come back, Condor was aghast. Hummingbird flew around Creator in a joyful frenzy, forward and backward, up and down and sideways, until she landed on the shoulder of Creator. Creator then turned to look at hummingbird and in a deep stern voice said, "Who is this that has the ability to fly to center of the Hanaq pacha, and who is looking me straight in the eye?"

"It is I, hummingbird, the smallest bird of your creation," she said proudly, as the shimmering red and green colors of her chest feathers, and her royal purple crown glistened in the golden rays of the Upper World. In delight, Wiracocha smiled and bestowed the title of Siwar Q'enti (see-wahr-kent-ee) upon his smallest of bird creations. "You are the first one to be able make this epic journey to very center of the Heavens, and you are the first one to have the courage to look me in the eye. Therefore, you are no longer hummingbird, you are considered Royal Hummingbird, Siwar Q'enti. And so, with honor, conceding his title of messenger of the Heavens, Condor is still considered the king of the skies, but hummingbird is the one who crosses the threshold, and is the bridge to the soul's message and the messages of the Heavens.

In the Andean Prophecy of the Taripay pacha, hummingbird is considered the carrier of the energies of this new initiation. Hummingbird is a symbol of regeneration and resurrection. Unlike the condor who is a scavenger and feeds on carrion, the hummingbird feeds exclusively on flower nectar, teaching us that when we feed from the sweetness and wonders of life, we are able to cultivate and bloom a delicate flower within our hearts that is full of joy and beauty. The nectar of life is produced from this flower within. Siwar Q'enti then seeks us out to drink of this essence, connecting us to the celestial, heavenly realms and the Divine Nature from which we are born.

Hummingbird assists in raising our frequency to match the vibrations of the Golden Age, and pushes us to the next level of consciousness and human evolution. Within hummingbird's figure eight wing pattern is the symbol of infinity. In hummingbird's ability to stop in mid-flight, with wings still moving, we are guided toward finding inner stillness while in motion in order move out of the finite and into the infinite. Through journeying into hummingbird essence and its unique qualities of flight, the hummingbird teaches how to transcend linear time and how to live and operate within the spiral nature of sacred time. Hummingbird reminds us that our soul is on a journey of epic proportions and to thrive on this epic journey we must feed from, produce within and share with others the nectar of life, becoming the People Made of Honey.

Connecting with our internal rhythm and inner wisdom

Each of us has a window during the day, or evening, when our energy is at its peak and we feel more connected, more inspired and more in our power. All of us have our own natural, internal rhythm and timing. Some are quick to move and accomplish tasks while others slower. Some go to University, get a degree and move into a job, then get married and start a family, while others are on a different track, taking years to travel and explore the world, before doing any of the aforementioned. We are all unique and have our own divine timing, and yet we are constantly being compared to others, or comparing ourselves and our outward accomplishments with what society defines as normal or successful. Stop doing this. You're suffocating your inner wisdom and you are suffocating your soul, while reinforcing the messages of mass enculturation, that society bombards us with. This is not what you came to do. You did not come here to become like someone else. You came here to discover you and to live that You to your fullest. The inner genius, described by Michael Meade, is the "Genius of the Soul". The resident spirit of the soul, present in each person, that has a unique way of seeing and engaging with life. The inner genius, is a combination of the inherent and unique gifts, talents, skills, desires, abilities, as well as the inner inclinations of style, that give shape to the soul within. The inner genius is connected to the inner nature of a person and that is connected to the eternal nature of life. When alive and well, our inner genius feeds us inspiration and keeps our lives fresh and flowing. However, to become one's unique self in the western culture, is not only like swimming upstream, but more like swimming through huge ocean waves of consensual reality. Mass culture does not support the development and freedom of the intelligence of the unique individual. The question becomes, can you awaken your individual uniqueness and learn how to live with it, becoming the undivided person, by being your true self? Being who you are, loving in the way you do, creating in the way you do and in your own timing, despite what those around you are doing or saying? Saying yes to your true self is committing to your highest purpose. We come into this world already being someone, with meaning embedded within us. We are born with purpose. In indigenous cultures when a child is born, there is a shaman or medicine woman who has been in touch with the soul of the child, and has received the messages of who this soul is, and what they've come to do. The information is given to the parents so the parents and the community know how to support the individual as they develop and grow. Supporting and celebrating the uniqueness of a child, while encouraging them to use their skills and talents, is a gift to not only the child, but to the entire world. Typically, the inner genius first awakens in youth as a strong interest in the arts or music, or as a desire to become someone or to follow particular vocation. Unfortunately, this inner calling is often squashed by society, ridicule or adult projections onto the child that make the them believe their dream is not possible. Maybe the doubt is due messages that they are not smart enough, talented enough, don't deserve it, or there's not enough money. Sometimes it's the most innocent comment made by another, at just the right time or in the right situation, and the inner genius absorbs the message and shuts down or hides.

The beautiful thing about our inner genius is that we can reawaken and invite this part of us forward at any stage of life, whether you are thirty, fifty, seventy or eighty years old. I've experienced this myself and have assisted many others in soul retrieval journeys where that most life affirming and innocent aspect of our soul comes back home and is made a full member of the person's life. From that point onward a path opened up and things began to change for them. When the spirit of our inner genius is alive and well, we are less available to depression and despair, less easily defeated and more consistently inspired and happy.

The ancients offer us some simple, yet profound practices to get back in touch with our uniqueness and our internal rhythm. The first step is to put yourself on notice. When we are out of touch with our bodies and our personal cycles, we will most likely be out of touch with Mother Earth and the cycles of nature. Without that connection to our internal needs and rhythms we will lose balance. Start observing the various levels of energy you go through in a day, when you feel your best and when you feel at your lowest. Notice when your energy is calmer, connected and make a point to carve out as much time as you can to sit quietly with yourself and to listen to your inner guidance. Even better is if you can be outside on the Earth during this time to absorb more energy and amplify your life force. When you find your window of peak connectedness, stop anything that is taxing and engage in something that brings you joy and feeds your happiness, even 20 minutes will do wonders. On the days that you have more time, find the places in nature that you feel especially connected with. Find the power places where energy is naturally stored and flowing through. Our bodies are electromagnetic, so when we go to a power place, focus our intention, and connect our energy there, the attention of Mother Earth will flow more strongly to that place and to the person/s who are there. Our energy bodies and internal rhythms will synch with energy of the place. We become a catalyzer of greater forces, leaving us more attuned, connected and revitalized. When seeking these places of power, it is not difficult. Ask your inner genius where he/she would like to go and ask them what they would like to do while there. Open your imagination and invite them. As Einstein once said, "Imagination is the doorway to genius." Make a playdate with your inner genius. Maybe they want to nap in sun and daydream. Maybe they want to read or draw or paint, play an instrument, or write. And perhaps they want to make a ritual. Wherever you go, remember to bring an offering of gratitude for the beauty and gifts you will experience. It could be anything, a song, a flower or a prayer. Whatever your offering is, bring it forth from your heart.

We each have a particular season of the year where we feel at our peak and most alive. Whatever this season or time of year is, it is a very good time to devote time to yourself and internal rhythm, to plan a retreat or a vision quest, to step out of your everyday life and into the Dreamtime.

We are in midst of an over turning of time, at the closing of an era and on the precipice another. We are experiencing enormous chaos and confusion as Earth's old templates release. And, this is a deeply mystical juncture as well, the beginning of a new cycle. With each new age or pacha comes new perspectives, new information, new potentials and new frequencies. Paradigms of the previous age either evolve or completely dissolve, if they are not in alignment with the evolutionary impulse. This pivotal point in creation is shaking everything up, making space for an entire new age to be birthed. We are each being asked to begin creating this new era from within, in alignment with the cosmic frequencies flooding through and infusing the ethers. This is not an easy task if we do not take the time to remove ourselves from the noise and congestion of our inundated busy lives. In preparation to receive the new energies, go to the mountain, go to the wilderness, or a secluded place where you feel deeply connected. Empty your mind and cleanse your energy field. Reset your internal rhythm with the rhythms of nature. Then vibrationally attune yourself with the information coming through you, as you are shown how to participate fully in the design of the new infrastructure, within and without, of the new era.

Shapeshifting

Another tool the ancients have left for us is the art of shapeshifting. Traditionally, shapeshifting is known as the rare ability to shift one's actual physical form into another form, typically into the totem or power animal or bird of the individual, through the energetic process of metamorphosis. This was a skill practiced and honed only by a few shamans of the past who had mastered the Law of Kollary. However, shapeshifting is still a relevant practice used in native cultures of today's age. Shapeshifting is not just about transforming into another form. One of its many gifts is being able to shift our energy and move into alternate realms of perception. The value of being able to shift into Eagle perception, for example, can lift us into a more expanded view of ourselves and our life circumstances, while reminding us what it feels like to be free, to be able to spread the wings or our spirit. Dancing and shifting into the level of Puma perception is a very powerful way to move us out of fear and into a calm, relaxed state of awareness, as Puma has no enemies. Through rhythmic sound, meditative movement, dance and breath, while imagining ourselves merging with the animal or bird, we can easily move into a different energetic state and state of mind.

In working with people who have no prior shapeshifting experience, I've found that for most it is a fun and effortless process that yields surprising results, new found energy and insights. Shapeshifting is an art that can awaken dormant energy centers and activate aspects of long forgotten instinctual aspects of our nature. Buried by an over domestication of our spirit, and ideas of what it means to be a civilized human in the western culture, the practice of shapeshifting aids in awakening innate gifts such as telepathy, clairvoyance, clairaudience and heightened intuition. All of which are intrinsic abilities just waiting to be turned on within each of us. On a day to day basis, learning to shape shift and move with the celestial and planetary currents of the day, is essential if we are to learn to flow in unison with this dynamic Universe and living energy system, we are so intimately one with.

From a vibrational view point, If no day is ever the same, and change is a natural law of the Universe, why would we fight so hard to remain the same person throughout our life, or try to control circumstances and outcomes to the point of exhaustion? I've often considered that perhaps one of the reasons people of a western mindset expend so much energy on staying in the familiar, is because they're attempting to find some solid ground in an otherwise fluid reality. The problem is when the solid ground or security, is falsely created through the over identification with the material world, a fixed time, or refusal to let go of what once was working in their lives, but isn't any longer.

On the shores of Lake Titicaca there is an ancient culture called the Aymara. Some say the Aymara are the oldest living people of South America and are the "Mothers" of the Q'ero. They live on floating islands made of reeds. Literally, everything is made from reed, their homes, boats and even their beds, and all of it is floating on the waters. No rock, or dirt or mineral substance as a foundation. Just plant material. When you walk around you can feel the bundles of reeds undulating beneath you as the currents of the water change with the wind. When I asked, "aren't they worried that their homes and belongings could easily get destroyed or washed away by a storm," I was told that the Aymara understand that the nature of physical reality is temporal, including their bodies, so why be worried. What a beautiful way to live I thought. Such trust in their connection with the Eternal.

I feel strongly that if we can learn to change, adopt more expansive mindsets and perspectives that are in align with Universal and Spiritual Law and the incoming energetic waves of the Golden Age, we will find ourselves living in totally different world, one where the emphasis is not placed so heavily on the material, but instead the emphasis is on our place and role within the Living Energy System.

Imagine for a moment that you are not limited to the form and identity you see when you look in the mirror. Imagine a portal opening in front of you. It connects you to your highest vibrational expression. Who are you? What are you? How do you dress? How do you move? How do you speak? What is the color and tonality of your energy? Let yourself play and explore these questions from time to time. It may just help you begin to shift your perception and the image you have locked yourself into, and have limited yourself to, based on the past, self-judgment or the social consensus.

Imagination is the doorway to new creations! By exercising the freedom of imagination, we open the field of unlimited possibility, and we draw new life to us and to those around us!

*"At the core of each of us is a unique tonality and frequency. We each
are an instrument through which creation sings her song. Clearing
the dissonance from our energy field is akin to tuning our instrument
and allowing ourselves to be played, while Great Spirit orchestrates
the perfection of the Universe through us." Chandra Sun Eagle*

Yuya

Yuya (you-ya) is the realization, on all levels of consciousness, of
the wisdom of power, and the perfection of the Universe. Beyond
the one-dimensional knowing of the mind, conceptual knowing
or intellect, the law of Yuya draws us into the realization, and
blueprint of universal perfection. The law of Yuya is not an easy
one to convey in words. As we are all familiar, the shamanic
path is one of revelation through direct experience. However,
I will do my best to provide you with some ways in which you
might start accessing this universal law. Within this realm of the
Kaypacha, or 3D reality, where all dimensions coalesce, there is
a creative perfection, that resides beyond the limiting perception
and field of duality, beyond the barriers of language, and
beyond the identification with beliefs and dogmas. Inside every
human being is Spirit, and all barriers can be overcome through
our work with Spirit and living in ayni. Creator's original plan
for humanity and the Pacha Mama is ayni, and within the field
of ayni, the wisdom and perfection of the Universe can be
experienced. It is the field where the soul, the heart and our
intrinsic nature converge in pure, sacred action. To realize Yuya,
the wisdom of power, the paqo must have clear perceptual filters,
and be able to turn information and knowledge into wisdom,
through humble acts of power. If not, information and energy
streaming from the Cosmos as Universal Wisdom, will get
trapped in the literal and in the personal. Clearing perceptual
filters, as mentioned earlier in Cheka, is the act of uncovering the

relative truths, stories, judgments, attachments and the illusions of the mind. In addition to having clear perceptual filters, Yuya is also attained through observation, stillness, detachment from the literal, and detachment from outcome. As the Paqo accesses these states she is able to harness more Kausay for co-creating her life, and organize reality at the essential (kollana), level of creation. The free flow of Kausay, which is the fuel and life force within all life, visible and invisible, and the free flow of Illya, which is pre-manifest, un-potentiated, primal life force, are key ingredients to accessing the spiritual law of Yuya.

For the Paqo, the wisdom of power is also about being able to make rain, without knowing the molecular structure of rain. Of equal importance to clearing our perceptual filters, is realizing our oneness with all life, and our own uncorrupted wisdom. We have to know that we are no greater than an ant, and no less than the divine. Medicine men and women perform miraculous healing, dissolve their form and turn into jaguars, owls and wolves, along with many other, seemingly impossible, feats from this very knowledge.

Understanding Yuya involves a remembering of our inner, un-corrupted wisdom and perfection. When I first heard this, I was very perplexed as to how one could tap into this state of consciousness, without physically dying. Fortunately, as with many of the techniques and methodologies found within shamanism, there is a way. It is a profound shamanic journey that takes us to time before we were born, the time before we incarnated into physical form, to the place where our Over Soul resides. This is a journey to the Center, the center within and without. The Over Soul resides in the upper dimension of higher frequencies, and is the part of our soul that remains in closest proximity to Source. Placed throughout the Andes there are certain portals through which we can make this journey. One such portal is the sacred place of Amaru Muru. It was here, through this doorway that I made conscious, energetic connection with the essence of my Over Soul. A potent journey that left me weak in the knees for a good hour afterwards.

Yuya and the Mythic Vision

The elders say that with a mythic vision that is in proper alignment, the Paqo and their community will experience "1001" fulfillments, over and over again, endless possibilities of abundance and life affirming experiences. A mythic vision is not a personal, ego-centric based vision. The common relationship to vision in the western world tends be more about the personal and is usually very "goal" oriented. In five years, this is where I want to be or this what I want to have or have accomplished. From this perspective, vision and true dreaming are limited, restricted and reliant on the cause and effect directive, that can also be subject to illusion. The mythic vision that the shaman aligns herself with is one of a collective, healed state. It is a vision that flows with synchronicity. It is an animated metaphor that reflects the qualities of joy and beauty, unbound love and truth, and is infused with the primal energy of creation. Paqos choose to participate with life based on sacred interaction and reciprocity with each other and the natural world. They understand that more important than what we do is this world, is what we become. Creating harmony within creates harmony without. They live and create from a place of wholeness, balanced in and with the feminine and masculine principles of creation. But it is not consensual reality that the shaman lives and acts through. Their proactive engagement happens at the mythic level, at the energetic, calibrated with a mythic vision of Munay, beauty and fulfillment for all life. Their vision is brought into manifestation through engagement with the essential and transpersonal qualities of creation.

We are all aware of the countless number of people that are working to create change for the better, such as environmentalist, teachers, artists, political activists, mothers, doctors, lobbyists and researchers looking for cures for cancer and other diseases, just to name a few. The problem is that most of these actions are taken only on the literal level and with an old perceptual and emotional state informing the doer. From a shamanic perspective, these people are re-creating a different version of the same situation and energetic signature that is calling for change. The old paradigm of fighting for change on the physical, without an energetic shift in consciousness and frequency perpetuates the problem we are desiring to change. Taking action in the world, no matter how good the intention, that is fueled with resistance, fear or anger in your heart, plants those very seeds of consciousness, and reinforces the old paradigms in morphogenic field.

To create something new, to re-write humanity's and the planet's future, shaman's say we have to drop the old doer and the old way of doing, so that all is left is the great action of Spirit. Dropping the doer and the doing is to first change the perceptual state from which we are coming. The second step is to align with the new mythic vision of the Golden Age, the time where the spirituality and sacredness of all life will be realized by all. Third, we must be able to embody an inner state of acceptance, and trust in divine order and peace. If not, our actions often arise from the old paradigms of judgment of good and bad, wrong or right. They will arise from thinking we need to fix something, need go to battle against the opponent. These are old views from old paradigms that were born from false education, our addiction to drama and the tendency to act from fear. There are no limits to your power when you align with Yuya, Munay and the mythic vision of The Golden Age. Your life and actions will spontaneously by inspired by peace, love and Spirit, and will be infinitely more potent in creating a new blueprint within the collective consciousness. Bring change to the world on the foundational energetic level that creates reality by changing your perceptions and beliefs.

Our availability to Spirit's plan

The Q'ero have a very interesting perception of time. They don't see our future as something existing in front of us and the past as something behind us. It's actually the opposite. The Q'ero experience the energies of our future as coming from behind us and enveloping us. They say we are the organizers of the past/future that is in front of us. What we create is based on our availability and receptivity to the future that flows from the past. When I first learned of this concept it took me awhile to understand its meaning. My mind, like most, had been programmed to think the future lies ahead and I need to envision it. When in fact, after looking back on my life, much of my life has not been about me creating the vision, it's been more of a journey of following the impulses of energy that were flowing through me. For example, I had no idea that walking the Andean Spiritual Path and becoming a shamanic practitioner and ceremonialist was part of my life path. It wasn't something I ever dreamt of or wished for. It all came to me, called me and summoned me because of one thing, my desire to understand the longing I felt inside. That's it. That one thing is what made me available to my future. It came in waves from behind me and enveloped me. The energies of my future flowed through with such intensity. I had two choices. To resist and fight, which I did do at times, or to surrender and flow with the currents and allow them to shape a new me and new reality. We are all shaped by life as much we shape our life. When I really contemplated this, I realized that any profound idea or impulse I've had, did not originate from my mind. Rather I made myself available and tapped into it. I used the desire of my heart and an open, receptive mind to be available for the inspiration and vision to come through me, but it did not come from me. We are not the original creators. But when we align with Light and make ourselves available to being of service to the greater vision and the impulses that are coming from Creator, we become the stewards and the co-creators of a higher order. The energies of the greater vision already exist in the fluid structure of the Quantum Field of infinite possibilities. This is what the visionaries mean when they speak of dreaming a new world into being. They first access the unified field and the frequencies that nourish life. Cultivating an unwavering connection with creative forces, they envision and breathe fire and passion into a framework of Light that becomes the container for the forces to manifest in the physical. They help organize the energies flowing through and to them. You can learn to do the same. Try loosening your grip on the future, become open and available to how Spirit and the future, flowing from behind, wants to inform, guide and direct you.

Much like the Native American tradition of Vision Questing, the Andean Paqo makes a vision quest or annual pilgrimage to their sponsor mountain to pray intently for support and guidance, to fortify their life force, the mythic vision they carry, and to recommit to their vows of sacred service.

Vision Questing should not be left to Paqos and shamans alone. Making a pilgrimage to a personal power place, while praying for vision and life direction in alignment with your personal gifts and purpose, can be embarked upon by everyone.

Becoming available to Great Mystery and connecting with the mythic vision of The Golden Age, and your personal participation with this vision, happens by parking the ego and entering stillness, through the window of the heart, journeying into the Unknown, into the Void, from which all life emerges and all life converges. The healed state and the creative instructions of how to bring this vision into being comes by sitting, communing with Creator and then calling the vision to you through the language of sound, chanting, the flute, the drum or any other instrument that you can pray through. Sound moves us into a realm beyond the mind, beyond words, and into the fluid, formless, pre-manifest, un-birthed potentiality of creation. Sound becomes the carrier wave of our heart's intentions and the purest form of resonant transmission.

Source, Perfection and Wisdom of the Five Elements

We've been speaking about realizing our full potential, connecting with a mythic vision and living that vision. The following is an example of how to work with the descending energy of Source as it manifests on this plane through the five elements, Ether, Air, Fire, Water and Earth. I was first introduced to this method of alchemy during my studies and training in Polarity Therapy. It has proven to be invaluable and in total congruence with Indigenous teachings. Indigenous people consider the Elements to be the Five Clan Chiefs that govern the physical realm and provide a platform for physical existence. Each element is a body of consciousness, inter-related with the others. Corresponding to our spiritual body, physical, mental and emotional bodies, each Element is a teacher and shaman. The following is a powerful practice of working with the Five Elements, to help you actualize your unique role, personal gifts and contribution to the New Era. When done consistently, this practice will give the creative life force within you a clear template and directive to follow. Enjoy!

This process may take a couple of hours and should be done as a ritual. So, make sure to have the time with no interruptions. Create your sacred space however you desire, and have a journal or piece of paper and pen next to you.

1.) The Element of Ether. To connect with Ether is to connect with Source Energy through our High Self, with the intention of connecting with the mythic vision of the Golden Age and your life vision/purpose enfolded within this mythic vision. Through silence we are able to hear our inner guidance and the voice of Spirit. Ether is the gateway in and out of manifest form, and connects us with the energy of the cosmos. Ether relates to spaciousness and expansiveness and the freedom to express. Residing in ether to be in full presence and is the basis for all profound visionary and healing work. To be in presence with yourself and the vision that wants to come through you is extremely healing. Get yourself out of the thinking mind and into a neutral, receptive channel. This is paramount and may take some time. Be patient and remember that practice is the key. Using meditation, shamanic breathing techniques or drumming are all great ways to enter stillness and get into a neutral space. Once you are in a deep place of calm and centeredness, connect with your heart, to your High Self, Spirit and your Inner Genius. Ask what it is that you most care about in life, what are your best and natural qualities and what brings the most inspiration, joy and juice to your life force. Trust what comes. As your heart speaks, write it down as single words that capture the essence of each vision or thought. Don't write in sentences. Spend as much time as you need here. Once you feel complete with this process, go through your list and circle the most potent 20 words on the page. Then go back into breathing and meditation for 5-10 minutes. Get into that empty, neutral place again. Then once again, open your eyes and circle only 7-10 of the 20 words that you already circled. These 7-10 words should carry the greatest weight in who and what you are really about. Don't think. Feel. Let your instincts guide you. Now you're ready to create the essence of your Life Vision Statement as an umbrella for all other ideas and creations to flow from. Keep in mind that this vision may shift and adjust over the years as you evolve. From those final words you're going to write a short visionary poem, adding as few words in-between your 7-10 essence words. I also suggest adding body movements and postures to match you vision statement and anchor it into the physical plane. It's a very fun process that will help you move into the feeling state of your soul vision while you speak or sing your poem each day. The Ether Element governs the throat chakra, the thyroid gland and the metabolism, joints and body cavities, as well as our sense of hearing.

2.) The next step is to work with the element of Air, which relates to the mental realm, thoughts and ideas. When your mental realm is clear, Air will express as quick thinking, agility of the mind, openness, innovation and possibility. Ether is to Air, as Spirit is to Mind. Once you've got the bigger picture and essence of your soul purpose and vision statement, which you will speak out loud, as many times as you need, until you've generated the coherent feelings associated with it, bathe in those feelings, and massage your yourself into a good feeling place. Then connect with the element of air, the wind, and your breath, while asking the following questions: what am I inspired to create at this time in my life that will support my soul vision? Is it writing? Is it art? Is it a workshop, a ceremony? Maybe you want to hold a gathering or help organize an event. Whatever it is - let the ideas flow. And be very cognizant of any undercurrent thoughts that make you doubt or second guess yourself. If limiting beliefs come up, remember they are from the subconscious programming and are presenting themselves so you can clear them. Air corresponds to the heart chakra, and as mentioned above, relates to our mental realm and nervous system.

3.) The Fire Element relates to our passion, vitality, exuberance and passion for life, the ability to focus our attention and to take action. With a healthy fire burning inside, we find ourselves inspired to use our will to set things in motion and feel confident to do so. Once you have decided on what idea and form of creation you would like to manifest, connect with the Fire, the flame of excitement and passion you feel around this idea. The question to ask here is: what do I need to do today or this week that supports this creation? What action steps do I need to take to get this idea in motion? Listen intently, but do not squeeze the energy by trying too hard. Relax into it. Don't be surprised if one of the answers that comes is to rest, relax, meditate, or go out into nature where you can day dream, imagine and feel into what your creation will be like. Sometimes doing nothing is exactly what's needed. Write down what comes immediately. Your heart and soul will speak clearly, concisely and most likely in short answers or through images. If the answers get long and complicated, most likely the thinking mind has clicked in. If this happens, go back into your breath and meditation until your mind is quiet. If you can't "see" how doing something is going to help, don't question it. Do it. Act on it immediately. If the answers are coming from your heart, they are coming from your inner wisdom, your innermost being and High Self. Signs of imbalance or a healthy relationship with fire will show up as lack of will, confidence or inability to act, typically associated with the 3rd, or solar plexus chakra.

4.) The Water Element, the great catalyst. Water is the flowing, merging, nature of relationship, nurturing, making connections, dissolving boundaries, cleansing, emotions and the Unknown. Water has the ability to flow around obstacles or wear them down over time. Water relates to emotions and needs Fire for warmth, Air for cleansing and Earth for boundaries. No heat and water freezes. Not enough movement or Air and water because murky. Water also relates to resource. Too much water and things drown. Too little water and life dries up. While connecting with a body of water, a stream or river, imagine you are in it and let yourself slip into its embrace. You are fully supported; let go into this support. Now, ask yourself: What resources do I need to support my vision and creation? What is that supports my dreams? This could be money, time, the support of others, collaboration, material things, or perhaps it's personal growth and a shift in perception that is needed. Does resource flow to me or is it blocked? Taking inventory of the resources and support in your life, and giving gratitude for it all, will open the flow for more to come. Working with Water is about receiving and filling your reserve tank, so you have what you need when the time calls for it. And again, if answers come that don't make sense to you, don't doubt them if they've come from your heart. Listen and follow. Imbalances or stagnation of Water can show up in the sacral chakra, an inability to connect with your creativity and Universal abundance.

5.) The fifth step, working with the Earth Element, is the final vibrational step down of Source energy, and is about bringing things into form and actualizing the vision. Earth defines boundaries, giving channels for Water, our resources, to flow in the right direction. When looking at your relationship to boundaries, the question becomes: what is the space and distance within a particular boundary? Is it a tight space? Is the boundary to confined, narrow or rigid? Or do you have to lose a boundary, with yourself or others, and energy is being leaked. Spiritually, Earth helps to anchor the Kundalini life force, otherwise it can rise too fast, with the potential of creating imbalances in the nervous system, energy body and mental realm. Working with Earth is where we get detailed about the structure, the plans, and what type of container and soil, our creation needs for its roots to grow deep. Staying grounded with our vision, so it can come to fruition, is to get organized and methodical. It is to persevere and stay steady. While grounding and connecting with Pacha Mama ask these questions: What does the structure or container, for my intentions and vision look like? When is it or what's the time frame? Where is it? Who's there? We want to get really specific. And, we have to let it go at the same time, not getting stuck in the exact way of how something will happen or how it will manifest. While we are disciplined with our plan and actions, we also have to be willing to let Spirit in and trusting that it if things do not happen exactly as we planned, that all is happening as it should and is in the highest. Don't squeeze creation and your vision, by gripping, holding or controlling. Earth is also about completions and the ability to release things when they have reached their final stages of form, not clinging and holding on when it is time to let something go. Imbalances in with Earth Element will often show up as issues in these areas of your life and in the root chakra.

Efficiency and Practicality

Here's another perspective on how to approach creating change through "mythic vision." How does the medicine person bring change to their life and to the world? They are proactive on the mythic level and they engage life at the energetic, at the essential, (kollana).

Another level of Yuya's teachings is about practicality and efficiency in life, through knowing the wisdom and perfection of the Universe and it's organizing principles. The power and first practical step of the medicine person is to access creation at the essential, as close to the origins or mouth the river as possible. For us this is the most practical and efficient way to work with life, to engage and employ the laws and frequencies of Spirit. Shamans do this by emptying the mind, detaching from the literal, and with embodied connection to Spirit and Natural Law, we set our intention to birth and create beauty and abundance for all. This is often called The Beauty Way or Walking the Beauty Path amongst native tribes of North America. There are medicine people all over the world that live and practice this way of life. They are the ones that have been weaving and maintaining the sacred fabric of creation for thousands of years, through their ceremonies and rituals, and work in the dreamtime.

This heart-centered way of living is the responsibility of the medicine person and this responsibility is to live with, and to create from the place of a Universal mythic vision in vibrational alignment with the approaching "Golden Age." The Paqo cultivates and preserves this alignment through the following responsibilities. First, we develop and maintain high level of awareness, while remaining available, through the open conduits within the mind and the energy body so that Spirit can come through. Availability for the Paqo, is an organizing principle that has to do with our degree of surrender. Our availability to Spirit is not based on conditions or conveniences. When Spirit calls the Paqo answers. Second, we maintain the inner wisdom of the mythic vision by remembering and honoring the old prayers, the power of the shaman's archetypes, the ancient ones and the luminous ones who have walked before us. We call them into our lives, source from their wisdom, and thus we keep their essence and knowledge alive and evolving. The third responsibility is to maintain and steward the new evolving myth of the "Golden Age" through luminous awareness and our energy medicine body. It is our responsibility to become the energetic embodiment of Ayni and the 7 Saiwas. Then and only then are our daily actions spontaneously in alignment with the highest good.

Within this body of responsibility, we find that there is a body of discipline, and practice that are needed to cultivate and maintain the framework of the new evolving myth. Many of these practices take us back into the teachings outlined in the chapter on Cheka. The first practice is finding and dropping the old familial and cultural mythologies that do not align with the new evolving myth of the Golden Age. Once a mythology, or paradigm, that is conflicting, we address it with love, track the imprint left by the old mythologies, then we heal the wounds, and transmute the limiting beliefs, while lifting the old mythology to a higher place. The second discipline involves finding the values of the new mythology and bringing these values into the world through our ceremonies, rituals and daily encounters within their communities. The fourth discipline involves selecting our commitments from the heart, and dedicating our life to the vision and intent that's revealed through this devotional practice. The Paqo brings all of this together by weaving the above four disciplines into the sacred geometry of their life and inspired action of service to all life.

Accessing the pure wisdom of Creation and becoming a catalyzer

We are all born from and are created from the image of a limitless Creator; therefore, we are all limitless co-creators ourselves. We stand between the heavens and earth with our physical body and energy body being fed and sustained by the energies of both. We are bridges for the celestial frequencies and the earth frequencies, but many have forgotten this or were never taught this. Awakening to this fundamental truth, and learning to access and employ our skills and talents, in the Beauty Way, way we become vessels that give and receive boundless amounts of energy simultaneously and automatically.

I hope the following inspires some understanding of how to access Yuya. This story is one account where I experienced Yuya in the natural world on a profound level. I have taken the principles learned through this experience and brought them into my daily life, through approaching everyday as a sacred engagement, and as an opportunity to know the creative potential of my uncorrupted wisdom. I also engage the wisdom from this experience as a reminder of the power within and the ability we each have to dream a new world into being, a new world created through the practice of mythic vision, and feeding the new guiding mythology of "The Golden Age".

The River Journey

Life is full of experience, but the meaning comes when we are able to find the teachings within each experience. In the summer 2005 I was hired to do shamanic healing and ceremony for group of a women that were traveling a 60 mile stretch of river in the Frank Church Wilderness of Idaho, over an eight-day period. I was to provide a couple of group ceremonies, spiritual teachings and individual healing sessions at the end of each day. Feeling very blessed for the opportunity I said yes. Unbeknownst to me, the eight-day journey turned into an extraordinary opportunity to practice the principles of Yuya, turning knowledge into wisdom. The first day of the trip was calm, the scenery was spectacular and the weather was beautiful. Falling asleep to the lull of the river dropped me into a deep and peaceful dream state that night. The next morning as I was just waking up, but still in that in between state of dreaming and waking when the following visions appeared. There was a Native American arrowhead and a stone from my mesa, which came from Machu Picchu, dancing around each other, as if they were trying to find alignment. And then bam, they aligned and a lightning bolt struck between them. At that point a second vision appeared. I was standing at the back of long canyon, high on the cliff side. Below me were hundreds of people standing in the valley. I heard a voice say, "the people are here, now teach them." I replied in my mind with, "teach them what?" Then the scene changed one last time. I was standing in a forest of trees, with a dirt path in front of me, and the voice spoke again, "make your point master." And with that I was snapped awake.

The river guide who rowed the oar boat I was riding on, I came to call the River Preacher. I named him this because his life was on the river, and as a general rule he said very little. When he did speak it was either a verse from one of Carlos Castaneda's books, a poem inspired by nature, or a story about the history of the land we were floating through, and the Native American People who once stewarded it. I was also quiet the first couple of days, as I sensed his discomfort with an unfamiliar person on his boat, trying to stay out of his way and offering a hand when I could. Because of this I earned some respect and towards the end of the second day he spoke his first words to me, other than, can you hand me that, and I prefer not to talk too much while on the river.

"So," the River Preacher said, "I watched you yesterday

when we got to camp, with your sage, singing and rattling, and making stone circles. Well, uh anyway......just" and then his voice trailed off. And that was it. That was all he said, but it was enough for me to understand he was aware and curious. The energy was high amongst the group and all were appreciating the wild. By the evening of that second day a big storm rolled in. The rain was heavy and at one point lightning struck a tree stump in the center camp, which sent everyone into a hysterical laughter of excitement and nervousness. The rain continued through the night, into the morning and throughout most of the next day. Despite the cold and damp weather, it felt great to be in wilderness and the women on the trip were not letting it get in the way of a good time. Smiles across their faces and with eagerness to get into dry clothes, the group arrived at camp those days in good spirits. But the following morning it was still cold and drizzly and it was starting to take its toll on the overall mood, including mine. About an hour into the day's journey, shivering and soaked, I said to the River Preacher, "I'm really not in the mood to sit in the cold rain all day. Are you?"

Without a moment's hesitation, he took one hand off the oar, turned to look at me and simply said, "well, can you do something about it?" For a few minutes I sat with his proposal and then replied with, "ok, let's see what happens when we both pray sun."

For a few minutes I contemplated what I'd learned from my teachers about when we are praying for something. Paqos and shamans pray in a very different way than most. We are taught that we are an integral part of the prayer, not just the words we use, but our very essence and our energy body are the key. For example, if we "pray for sun", we are taking ourselves out of the equation, we have separated ourselves from our infinite wisdom, and we are asking for the sun to come out at some point. When we "pray sun", as opposed to "pray for sun", we are stepping out of the literal, out of literal time, out of duality.

and into Kollana, the level of the essential energies and energetic exchange within creation. To move into the level of kollana, we must shift our vibratory state into the resonant field with the very thing we are desiring. This aspect of Yuya is what the Paqo refers to as the wisdom of power.

I quieted my mind and connected my consciousness with the environment and with the storm. Seeing the thickness of the clouds and how far they overstretched the land, I recognized a subtle undercurrent of doubt running through my mind. I redirected my attention to the possibility of it happening. Back and forth I went in my mind, until I remembered the essential component to prayer of becoming and feeling what I was praying for, which helped move me out of my mind and into my body. Generating the feeling of being warm and in the sun not an easy task to accomplish, as the rain continued to seep through my supposed waterproof jacket. My ability to concentrate and stay with my internal climate, despite my outside surroundings was proving to be quite a challenge an exercise in witnessing the errors and limits of my subconscious, as they rose in opposition to my mission. Deciding I needed to scale the task back from the entire sky being cloudless, to just the sky above the river being cloudless, and our boat in the sunshine as we floated for the next 10 miles, I settled my awareness on the most current memory I had of a warm day spent lying on a sunny beach, and relaxed into the feeling of warm, liquid sunshine flowing through my body for 15-20 minutes. My inner state shifted dramatically, but when I opened my eyes to see what was happening in the outside world, nothing had changed. I closed my eyes for another few minutes of imagining, then closed with a prayer of gratitude and let go of the outcome. About thirty minutes later, much to my surprise, the rain ceased, the clouds lightened and rays of sunshine were streaming through.

Extremely grateful, but not convinced that I had anything to do with the change, I left it as a possibility and turned my attention to the pristine nature around me.

That night I lead the group through a Despacho Ceremony. We all placed our prayers in the gift bundle and offered them to the Mother Earth and Great Spirit as we placed our prayers in the fire. It was a beautiful evening that created a sacred atmosphere and stronger bond amongst the women.

The next day was full of sunshine and loads of laughter. Six days in the on the river, in untouched wilderness, had all but washed away the stress and memories of the busy city lives that most of them led. I personally was pulsing with so much life force and gratitude I could hardly contain it.

On the second to last morning I woke to a quick flash of the dream images that came through at the beginning of the trip. I had very strong feeling that something unusual was going to happen that day. Once the camp was taken down and both oar boats were loaded, the River Preacher and I pushed off for another day of camaraderie and magic. Late in the morning the Preacher started telling me about our next campsite, describing a lightly worn, narrow, creekside trail that led to a small canyon above the campsite. Once in the canyon the seeker could find pictographs of Geronimo's story drawn on the rock walls. He also described a large flat stone just in front of the main rock wall, which he thought to be a ritual stone. As he spoke my awareness drifted in and out of time, and goose bumps popped up all over my body. Chills ran up and down my spine as he spoke. In addition to the special nature of the next campsite, the River Preacher, felt it necessary to forewarn me about trickiness of the outtake, "Just before the point of tie up, we will go through a large set of rapids, quickly make our way towards the left bank and then stick the entry. The space between the canyon walls on either side of the river form one, narrow passage way through that section of rapids. The narrowing of the canyon results in an increase in water force and speed." The Preacher was nervous. "If we miss the landing, which will come just after the rapids, we are screwed. That is our only opportunity. So, when I say jump, I want you to take this rope, jump to the shore and, as quickly as possible, tie the rope to the nearest boulder or tree you see. Got it?" For me, all of this was another sign of the area's sacredness. Indigenous people often sought out the most obscure and hidden places to establish their villages and conduct ceremony.

We made it through the rapids quickly and over to the left bank, and before I knew it the River Preacher was yelling, "Take the rope. Take the rope. Now jump." The boat was skimming the rocks on the shore line, but we were still moving at a good clip, when I heard a final, "Jump, damn it!" Together, we both jumped in unison, scrambled our way to the biggest and nearest boulder we could find, and got our boat and tied off, just as the second gear boat was coming in for a bumpy landing. It was a mad rush of excitement, but we were able to help them tie off. I caught my breathe and then grabbed my duffle and few other things and headed up the short, but steep trail to the plateau where we would set up camp. Reaching the top, I looked around briefly and spotted a place on the edge of the plateau where I would have privacy, and set up my tent. I still had a couple of hours before the group would arrive at camp, so off I went looking for the trail that lead to the story of Geronimo. As I walked around, I heard some rustling in the bushes, but I couldn't see anything. My attention was drawn to small pieces of trash on the ground and a subtle, but heavy energy in the area, so I went back to my tent and got my sage, Florida water, and rattle. I walked the entirety of the plateau, smudging, saying prayers and picking up the bits of trash I would find. I prayed to the spirits of the land, asking for their forgiveness of our disrespect of the land, and ignorance of our actions. I prayed to the four directions, above, below and within, and then built a medicine wheel out river stones. The hucha lifted and I felt a restored balance of energy of the area, so I closed with a prayer to the Mother Earth and guardian sprits, and asked if my work was complete. Hearing only silence, I didn't get the sense there was anything left to do at that moment, and headed back to my tent to change clothes and lie down for a moment. By this time, I only had half an hour or so before the others would arrive, and I would do my two last healing sessions of the trip. Just as I laid down a very loud rumble jolted me to my feet and propelled me outside. The rumbling sound reminded me of an earthquake, but I felt no shaking of the ground. Then I noticed the River Preacher standing on the south edge of the plateau that over looked the river, hands folded over the top of his head and staring up. I followed his gaze to the other side of the river. What I witnessed was incredible. I have witnessed an avalanche on Salkantay, and have been in the rush of a small avalanche while heli-skiing. As a small child I was knocked off my feet when lightning struck the ground twenty feet away from where I stood. I'd come across a bear, rattle snakes and bob cats while hiking, had a mountain lion run across the trail, just thirty yards in front of me, but never had I seen what I was bearing witness too in that moment. Right in front of our eyes, Mother Earth was shaking loose one single boulder, approximately 8-10 feet in diameter, from the top of the canyon wall across the river. In total awe, my body shook with electricity as the huge boulder, hundreds of feet up, finally broke loose. Rolling over and over on itself, barely disturbing any other stones or touching any trees along the way, it took one final bounce off the canyon wall and flung itself into the middle of the river, sending a wall of water some thirty feet into the air. Then all was quiet. We both stood in awe. The River Preacher walked to where I was standing. Breaking the silence and with a long steady glance, he turned to me and said, "I've been guiding on rivers most of my life, and I gotta say, I have never seen anything like that." He paused and with a twinkle in his eye, said, "A path without a heart is no path at all. You walk a good path and it seems this is recognized by a higher force." He gave me hug and whispered thank you in my ear, then turned and made his way back to the others. To me, the spirits of land and the Mother Earth had sent me a sign, a thank you in their language, for the energy I had cleared and for honoring the sacredness of the place.

Minutes later the women arrived and I moved into the last two sessions of the trip. Towards the end of the last session I sensed the same presence I felt when upon our arrival, in the bushes behind me. Every few minutes I saw a figure out of the corner of my eye. The presence was that of a native man and it seemed he was trying to get my attention. I finished the session and was about to go get some dinner, when I heard the rustling in the bushes again and his undeniable presence. Over taken by the feeling that I should get my mesa and head up the creek to the small canyon where Geronimo's story was recorded, I skipped dinner and did just that.

As I walked towards the trail my awareness heightened. The crickets were chirping, the air was soft and the sound of the creek felt like it was running through me. I felt no separation between me and the land around me. It took a great deal of mental effort to feel myself. Kneeling at the beginning of the trail, leaving some tobacco on the ground and asking for permission to enter, I heard man's voice say, "get off your knees. The offering is appropriate, but we called you, so you have permission." He was clear and stern. Slowly, I made my way along the creek and up the path until I was deep in the canyon, standing before the large flat stone the River Preacher had described. My eyes moved beyond the flat stone to the canyon wall in front of me. There it was, the story of Geronimo. Through extra-sensory hearing, I could faintly make out voices of women and children. As I listened, my vision shifted and I could see native women singing while they made food and built fires. I could also hear the voices of men in council. Then I heard the voice from earlier. "Thank you for coming. First, we want to give you a healing. Lie down on the rock. We wish to show you our gratitude." I placed my mesa and rattle on the ground, climbed onto the large stone and laid down on my back. A wave of potent energy washed over me immediately, altering and expanding my perception even further. The hands of two native women, on either side of me, moved through my body, smoothing and caressing my energy field, as I drifted into a deep state ease and grace. A spirit eagle flew down and landed on my chest and mountain lion came to my side. "Eagle comes to you so your heart can soar with vision. It will fly with the condor already with you. Mountain lion comes to walk by your side and to teach you how to lead. Now stand up and open your mesa. You will know what to do." Standing up slowly I lifted my mesa to the four directions, above and below, and then placed it on the flat stone. I knew immediately what to do. I took my serpentine stone from Machu Picchu out of my mesa and then walked to canyon wall in front of me. Staring at the symbols and pictures, I had the sense to walk right. And then I saw it. There it was, the exact arrowhead from my dream vision earlier in the week.

"We would like you to call in the Ancestors of Peru," said the spirit voice. The stone in my hand began to pulse and my hand quivered. Without any effort on my part, the stone was being magnetically drawn to the arrowhead on the wall, pulling my arm along with it. As powerfully as possible, I called to the ancestors of the Andes and to the Apu Kuna, calling each high altar by name, one by one. I felt I was in both places at the same time. A warm rush of energy came through my body and a strong wind blew up the canyon. Feeling weak in the knees, I sat down to ground myself. Peace filled my heart as the ancestors of North and South American came together in council. To this day I do not "know" the full spectrum of that meeting in the canyon, but I had a strong knowing that there was healing and balance happening, both on the earth and in the unity consciousness grid that surrounds the earth.

I stayed for a while longer, reading the ancient stories painted on the wall until I felt it was time to go. I gathered my things and said a silent thank you. My heart was so full. In reply, the native spirit who had summoned me said, "We thank you. For without the help of the human spirit we cannot bring harmony to the worlds. Do you understand? Will you accept more responsibility?" Not knowing what that would entail, I bowed in honor for being chosen for such service and let out a loud, "yes, I do!"

I walked back down to camp, had a late bite to eat and headed to my tent to get some rest, but I was way too excited and had way to much energy running through me to sleep, I laid there for some time going over in my mind, the amazing events of the day, eventually realizing that trying to sleep was pointless, so I got up and walked down the steep trail away from camp, and took a seat on a large stone at the river's edge. The night sky was clear and brilliant. The Stars were twinkling back and forth in a sequence of celestial code. In total bliss I sent a prayer to the heavens, "Can you please send me a sign that I have heard and interpreted today's earlier events correctly? That the ancestors of this place and Pacha Mama are pleased? I was asking less from a place of doubt, and more from a place of wanting to still play in the magic and wonder of the moment.

What happened next was absolutely extraordinary. On the night's horizon, lightning danced in the East Sky. I turned slowly towards the South to see the same phenomenon. I could hardly believe what I was witnessing as I continued to turn clockwise, landing in the West direction, lightning in the Heavens was answering me back and I was not making it up. It was as real as the stones beneath my feet. Taking a big breath I turned to the fourth cardinal direction. The Ancestors of the North were performing their magic in unison with the other directions, as bolts of electricity shot across the sky. I stood mystified and speechless under the perfection of the sky above. To this day, I have shared this night with very few people. I have kept it close to my heart.

The following day proved just as beautiful as the day prior, except for one slight challenge. There was a strong wind blowing up canyon, head-on, which was making it difficult to maintain boat speed. When this happens, not only is it more work for the oarsman, but because of the slower speed, your boat is at the mercy of the river, increasing the possibility of flipping more probable. The River Preacher was obviously nervous as he told me the story of his last journey through this section of the river. His boat had flipped in the last technical session before take out. He was thrown from the boat and was not able to grab a rope before the boat got away from him, leaving him with the only choice to swim the river in hopes of finding his boat. He said he swam a couple of miles before finding his boat top down, lodged between two shoreline rocks and half his gear missing, and he did not want to go through that again. Nor did I. I made sure my life jacket was close by and asked him if he could let me know in time to put it on. "I won't have to tell you. You'll hear it."

We floated through the calm section of the river at a slow pace, as the winds forced the River Preacher to work with all the strength he could gather. I could feel his agitation and tension mounting as the approaching rapids grew in size and their roar became louder. When we hit the second major hole, I was clutching the metal frame with all my strength, as the boat tipped onto one side and out went the River Preacher. Fortunately, he managed to hold on and not totally abandon ship. Eyes wide with disbelief and the fear of losing my captain, I made my way from the back of the boat to him, shouting for him to hang on. Feet and legs dangling in river with one remaining hand on the left oar, and using the other hand to try to pull himself back in the boat, while the other oar was getting tossed around by the river. "Grab the oar. Grab the oar," he was shouting, "lift it out of the water. Otherwise we'll spin." Stumbling over gear, half on my knees and half on my belly I managed to make my way to the oar and lift it out of the river. The preacher somehow pulled himself back in the boat and with a big yank, stripped the second oar from my hands, which sent me flying on my back to the bottom of the raft. A few moments later we were off the roller coaster and back in smooth waters. We relaxed for a while as the river meandered through the canyon, both of us quiet and counting our blessings. The wind had calmed. I couldn't help but think that the Preacher's anxiety and the fear he held from the past was having an effect on his river guiding abilities. Our time to relax ended another hour or so down the river, when the Preacher's mood revved back up. The winds had strengthened again. Looking at me with a very serious tone, the Preacher asked if I could do with the wind what I'd done with the rain six days prior. I explained in a patient manner that I did not know if I had any effect on the weather that day. He was not having it and with a desperate plea, asked if I could please try. I agreed and asked him to do his part by letting go of his anxiety and visualizing us making it through successfully. He nodded in agreement and I closed my eyes and went to work.

I began with a prayer, "Grandfather wind, I come to you with great request. I thank you for your grand presence and many blessings, but right now we and the rafts behind us, need to pass through this next section of the river safely. Can you please calm yourself so we and the others can reach our outtake safely." I kept praying, and as I prayed the wind began to calm a little. I heard the Preacher say good job. What you're doing is working. Excitement welled within and Grandfather wind mirrored my energy with swirling more strongly. Noticing the correlation, I quieted myself and went back into prayer. "Grandfather Wind, how do I do this? Teach me please." At that point a voice outside of myself spoke, "BECOME WHAT YOU WANT ME BE. DON'T PRAY FOR IT. BECOME IT!" Become what you want me to be? How do I become a soft breeze? The answer came immediately from within. The air element relates to our mental realm. Stop praying and go into silence. I invoked the feelings of a warm summer day. I let my mind go, as I held the feelings of a soft breeze caressing my skin, only to find myself back in thought moments later. Slightly frustrated, but fascinated by the corresponding wind patterns as I drifted in and out of mental stillness, until I eventually dropped into a deep quiet. Floating on the awareness of my own inhale and exhale, my body and mind became still. Grandfather wind seemed happy with the lesson and faded himself into gentle breeze that made only the smallest of branches sway in his breath. It had happened. The wind was calm and our speed was good as we dropped into the mouth of that giant wave, nose down and butt up. I remember feeling all the tension that had built up in my root chakra release, like someone had pulled out the stopper. The nose of the boat crested the peek and the back of the boat dropped into the pit. All I could see was the face of a giant wave bending our boat backwards, and all I could do was surrender to the moment and ride the rolling river.

The untamed river is a great metaphor of life. There are natural rhythms of floating along calmly followed by an increase in momentum, a wave of inspiration. We feel good, we have vision and our dreams and goals are taking form. Inevitably, events that are out of our control happen and toss us into the pit of a wave. We get water in our nose, we choke on the emotional upset, and get confused, fearful or frustrated because just last week or just yesterday, everything was going so well. We lose sight of the river ahead and can't seem to get back "on top" of our life. Many times, I have experienced such waves. While in the belly of the moment I have taught myself to relax, stay present and to trust in the perfection and wisdom of the moment, no matter how challenging. Difficult as it may be in those moments, we must remember that waves are a natural part of life and our soul's journey. The crest of the wave symbolizes the clarity of vision that comes while being at the vantage point and the trough of the wave represents bringing the vision and new information into our daily life and applying it. That entire river journey was the crest of a giant wave for me, and then it was my practice to go back into my daily life and apply the teachings experienced during that epic adventure. Learning to ride the waves of our life circumstances while holding integrity and peace is an ancient key to riding the ascending wave of evolution, as the Pacha Mama and all her children spiral through the Milky Way and into another phase of creation. Learning to trust in the perfection and wisdom of the Universe, while humanity goes through this purification phase will help us to stay in our hearts, while preparing to receive the immense wave of luminosity of the Golden Age.

Unlike speculations that this New Age will come all it once, it is rather a series of progressive events that are pushing us forward, and providing us with stepping stones into the "Heart of Oneness and sacred living - the wisdom and perfection of the Universe."

So, when praying sun, praying peace on Earth, or praying anything else you wish to see manifest in the world, remember that visualizing is good, but it's only a portion of the equation. You must become peace. You must become Light. You must attune your vibrational frequency and beliefs with what you wish to see manifest in the world. Being centered in the sacred within your own body, while remembering the uncorrupted wisdom of your origins, and maintaining connection to the purity and oneness of the divine perfection of the universe, and it's organizing principles will position you in the center of your co-creative potentiality. Remember to always begin your prayer with, remain and end in a state of humility and gratitude, and remember to apply the disciplines mentioned earlier in this chapter, of creating from the place of "mythic vision 1001 fulfillments of beauty and abundance for all."

"As we experience and perceive the Divine in all, we realize we never alone, rather we were under a trance and spell of separation from all that is." Chandra Sun Eagle

Chullya

Chullya (chew-ll-ya) is the Law of Unity, Oneness, communion and inter-connectedness. Everything that exists in the Universe, seen and unseen, is connected. Nothing is isolated. The principle of Chullya provides us with a guiding light for moving from duality and into an experience of communion with all that is, with our inner-connectivity, inter-dependence and unity with all life and the living matrix of creation. All other Universal laws are contained within the Law of Oneness.

In order to create and express, the One must divide itself, therefore the One, the Creator is within all life. It is from Oneness that creation divides to express itself through the multitude of manifestations that originate from Source. Oneness is spoken about in all spiritual traditions and is perceived as being an undivided, unified field of energy or web of existence. Separation and division are not our inherent nature. Unity is. This unified field of energy that we are all connected through, has its origins in Source or the Great Mystery, and this point of origin, the Source of creation is found within every part of the whole. We are all connected to and through the earth's electromagnetic field as well.

For the spiritual adept and shaman, Chullya establishes the journey of our destiny, the communing with all that is, the Creator's creation. We are united by the spirit of the Divine within each of us. Through this communing the shaman knows herself as One with everything. She is then able to participate with the great unfolding of creation from a place of wholeness and at the quantum level. For the Paqo, communing with creation leads to an embodied experience of our totality and connection with the Divine, while anyone, no matter where they are on their journey, having an experience of communion with the Light of Creation, no matter how long or short, will spark a seed of knowing a greater truth. In the Andean tradition of healing one of the first things that is done to restore wellbeing to the patient is to reestablish a clear channel and connection between them and the Light of Creator.

We have reached a point in our collective human experience and evolution where if we don't change our way of living and our way of thinking we may not survive. If our consciousness does not take form in Unity Consciousness and Spiritual Consciousness, we will not evolve. Humans have also reached a point where the Divine physical patterns have unfolded and have expressed themselves to their fullest potential within the 3D realm of existence. The next phase of our evolution will come through expansion of our consciousness into our cosmic existence beyond the limitations of the three-dimensional physical plane. We are now at the genesis of a new phase, a return to our origins, back to Oneness. This is the journey of returning Home.

Moving from material focus to an expanded view through the lens of the Unified Field connects us with something greater than our singularity, greater than our physical body and material attachments. Our hearts, bodies and minds begin to resonate and pulse different tones of frequencies that are associated with the Joy, Peace, and Trust.

So how do we come back into a state of communion, Oneness with all that is? Where do we begin? Just as we cannot truly know the meaning of Munay and unconditional love for others if we do not love ourselves, experiencing our oneness with the world is generated by feeling at One with our Self, all levels of our being and at One with Spirit. This great reunion with Creator and the Divine is ultimately achieved through the journey of

Life, where the communion with one's three fundamental bodies or levels of consciousness are connected, integrated and aligned. The Inner Wisdom represented by the Serpent, that rises from the underworld and out of the subconscious and into the Light of Wisdom and higher consciousness. The conscious Self, represented by the Puma and the full embodiment of awakened co-participation with and in our lives. The High Self, represented by the Condor, is third aspect of our soul that has evolved, is immortal and transcendent.

We will never experience transcendent states of Oneness through the thinking mind. Instead we have let go of everything we think we know and learn to embrace the Great Unknown through the wisdom of the Heart. Our DNA and High Self Consciousness contains within it the codes of Oneness. The High Self knows its oneness with all that is and It recognizes itself as one with Creator and creation, thus an essential part of living in the truth of our Divine Oneness requires a continual communion with our High Self. The shamanic traditions and mystical teachings of the Andes that lead to our eternal self and communion with oneness are often found through our connection with the natural world. The western mind set is mostly conditioned towards duality. Being in nature is one of the easiest ways, and purest portals to enter transcendent states beyond duality. The opposing forces of illusory separation and duality, tend to come from the over identification with the material that keeps one from knowing their inter-connectivity. It's not that we get cut off, or have been separated from the unified field of Oneness, it's that we lose the "awareness" of unity consciousness and therefore the feeling of it. When we are imbalanced and overly invested in the material world, our attention and our energy end up collapsing into singularity and into the finite. Over time, fear, stress and continually living in survival mode that binds our energy to a limited view of what is possible and what isn't possible.

Our challenge is to lift out of this trance of illusion and overcome the barriers that keep us oriented towards this way of perceiving. Connecting with Spirit and our High Self opens new portals of awareness that lead to an awareness that we are more than what we have been conditioned to think we are. Understanding that we are spirit beings in a human form is paramount. Alignment with this truth has the power to dissolve the divisions created by the illusion of separation, and our perceptions of self and the world around us begin to shift toward unity consciousness. Dissolving into Oneness we become nothing and everything at the same time!

The unified field or quantum field, is a field of information and infinite possibilities of creation's patterns. There is a limitless and endless stream of potentiality. We are part of this Oneness and are thus full of potential. From the Andean perspective our potential will rarely be actualized without participating with the world around us. We each have gifts, talents, skills, abilities and a unique Divine expression that is needed for the whole of life to thrive. I hear from many people, and know for myself, that when we feel a part of something bigger than our individual self, we have a sense of belonging, and this is a very important aspect to feeling and experiencing the Oneness within. It helps us understand our place and role within the web of life, and our service within the world. We learn about ourselves and discover things we may not have known or been able to see about ourselves when we are in a group or community.

On the other hand, for those who are always in the presence of others, feeling most comfortable when distracted or busied with activity, it is essential to spend time in solitude, preferably in Nature. Isolation from the outside world for periods of time, with the intention to connect to oneself and with Spirit is key to experiencing your Oneness. Communion through meditation, taming the mind and entering the window of stillness is and will forever remain an essential practice on all paths to awakening. Experiencing states of Oneness brings us into a feeling of euphoric bliss and connectedness, at One with everything. When we become aware of the quantum field through awareness, rather than through the physical, we enter wholeness. Our heart and our brain begin to function in more coherent states. Our heart and thoughts can begin to harmonize with and through the Natural, Organic Universal Laws and principles. From this state of awareness and place of existence, the power to change our life is in our hands. It is here that we begin to understand, exist and live from a more relaxed place of trust. We become more comfortable in the unknown and in the mystery of life, perhaps even excited about the unknown, as opposed to fearing it, because we feel supported by the totality of the universe. Living and creating in the unified field of information and possibility, we move beyond duality, beyond the measure of time and space, where miracles and instantaneous healing happens.

Chullya also outlines the practice of developing alignment in our thoughts and actions, with heaven and earth, so that our energy is no longer invested in, or subtracted by, opposing forces and selfish thinking. Thought is of great value when it is attached to intent and followed by immediate action. Chullya is about putting our compassion into action. When our thoughts are random, unconscious and repetitive, they take us out of the present, out of connectedness and out of oneness. Chullya, communion and congruence of thought, yachay, and action, llankay, with Heaven and Earth, and Munay, is essential so that our energy is no longer invested in, and diminished by the seductions of egocentric thinking.

The medicine person uses thought for contemplation, for learning. Awareness of where thoughts are originating from results in an ability to shift the thought form, belief and or complex, so that a new way of viewing the world and our life can be set into motion. Continuing to view personal and collective situations from the same level of mind and same perspective results in a collapsing of the quantum field of possibilities into a single point of view. We end up collapsing ourselves, ultimately into a very small and limited version of our potential. When we let go or suspend that point of view, the field of possibility opens back up, we open back up and new energy begins to flow to us. In order to attain new levels of consciousness, we have put aside our current state of understanding and framework of thought.

The Chakana - A bridge to Chullya

The ancients taught the spiritual laws and esoteric teachings, through sacred geometry, symbols, numerology, astrology, and mythology. The chakana or Andean Cross means bridge, and is found carved in stones at all ceremonial sites throughout the Andes, most commonly seen with four points, and three steps between each of the four steps. It is the most sacred symbol within Andean Mysticism, symbolizing the communion with, and the full integration and harmonization of energies of the four directions, the three worlds; the Hanaq pacha (upper world), Kay pacha (middle world) and Ukhu pacha (lower world), and our three fundamental bodies, of the High Self, Conscious Self and Unconscious, the three primary powers of munay, yachay and llankay. The layers of meaning and teachings within the chakana are multi-tiered and multi-faceted, providing a lifetime of instruction. Similar to the medicine wheel of North America, we are always traveling the spiral nature of the chakana. The number four represents foundation, the four quadrants of the Taywantinsuyu (the Inka Empire), and the four cardinal directions. The pathways and teachings of each direction on the chakana can be considered pillars and doorways that lead to the center, the Chaupin (chow-peen). Let's take a quick journey around the chakana.

The East

We turn to the East to align ourselves, our bodies and spirit with the Sun, the energy behind the Sun and the element of Fire. The East is the birth place of the medicine person, the peaceful humble warrior/warrioress that carries the sacred flame. We draw into us the sacred fire to feed our electrical body, spiritual body and galactic body. We commune with the East to ignite the passion and sacred fire within. Facing the East, we offer ourselves to life and step into being in service to Light and to Life. When our spirit is in true connection, we will know what to do and how to help, hence, each morning we face the rising sun to align ourselves with the new day and the prophecy of the day. And it is with the Light of the East that we activate our DNA, open the pineal gland and awaken consciousness. The original instructions from the Sacred Fire of the East are to stay close to the fire, feed it with all our life experiences, trials, tribulations, dreams and disappointments, pains and joy. All of it is fuel for the sacred flame within. Give it all to the fire for transmutation. And don't let the fire go out!

The South

The South is the door to reconnecting with the Tree of Life and the Earthly codes of our essence. This is where we learn to walk the Earth softly, in beauty and grace, as an Earth Guardian. Turning to the South we commune with the healing plants and become their custodians and the gardeners of Pacha mama's abundant garden. We nurture and feed our physical bodies with the energy of wellbeing, and fertility alive within the Pacha Mama. Entering the South door requires walking in a serpentine way, becoming one with the plants and stone people. While listening to them and the rivers and trees we are given the original instructions of how to live on the Earth in the Beauty Way, how to live in respect and reverence for our bodies and the bodies of all earthly creatures. When we turn to the South, we bring the Sacred Fire of the East with us. We smoke the sacred pipe and connect ceremonial sites, altars and temples with our walk and connect with the Wisdom of all Ages.

The West

Walking into the West, the East is at our back. Following the path of Light into the close of the day, as Puma swallows the Sun whole, we journey into the Mist, the Mystical Realms and into Mysteries of the Feminine through the medicine ceremonies. The west is a journey into what is hidden from us. We call to the water pourers in the West and ask to be blessed and cleansed of emotional and energetic debris. To enter the West, we are required to leave the material world behind us and enter the Great Unknown, where secrets and life essence within the waters of are found. The West teaches us how to adapt to all circumstances, how to go inside and heal, and learn to ebb and flow with the natural rhythms rather than attempting to manipulate. It is in the West that we will be shown if we are in the wrong river, the river of illusion, or the river of Truth. When we journey into West, into that which has been hidden from us, we can flow back into adaptation with the Truth. The West pillar also teaches how to care for the Waters, how to treat it so sacredly. Travel your lands and find the Source of water, the springs where Light and Air first touches the emerging waters. Make offerings and remember that all life comes from water and is born from the Pakarinas. Ask to be given the original instructions of water. Listen through the universal language of Light.

The North

The North door brings us into communion with the Elders, the Gray Hairs and the Wisdom Keepers. It is here that we call to spirit beings of the Light and make energetic connections with them. When our connection to North pillar is strong, we have a direct line of communication to the spirit world. They hear us and show up in our life and in our ceremonies. The North door teaches us how to breathe again, the shamanic breath of our spiritual essence and the breath of the winged ones. Sitting with the Wisdom Keepers we prepare our wings for flight, are reminded that we are spirit beings going through a physical experience. We are reminded that when this truth becomes our guiding consciousness, life becomes a joyous celebration. The North pillar's instructions guide us in how to recalibrate our thoughts and words so that our co-creations are shaped by wisdom and Spirit. We learn to let Spirit take hold, and we assume the responsibility of breathing life into what Spirit has disseminated through the sacred vision. Climb to peak of the mountain, high above the noise of the cities, where the air is clean and call to the gatekeepers of the ancient wisdom. Listen for the voices in the wind that carry the original instructions of how to bring your spirit essence into the world and how to carry forward the wisdom of the Elders.

On the chakana there are three steps between each of the four faces. These steps represent the three worlds and the archetypal trilogy, the Serpent, Puma and Condor. The Four directions plus three steps equal seven. The number seven is the point of equilibrium and Self Realization. The number seven of Self Realization is also represented in their flag, which is a rainbow, symbolizing the seven rays of frequency within the Rainbow Light Body. If you draw a line from each of the four vectors you will see a diamond shape. The Diamond geometry symbolizes the highest level of conscious, or the Diamond Code Consciousness and our Galactic Nature. You will see this symbol woven into the textiles, and the clothing of the Q'ero. Another interesting symbol you will see in some of the ancient temples, is that of plumed serpent with a puma head, representing the self-fulfilled and self-realized human. As I spoke briefly of in the beginning of this book, symbology, sacred geometry, effigies of birds and animals, and constellations saturate the lands, hill sides and mountains of the Andes. The evidence of the Andean living cosmology mirrors Heaven on Earth and unity with all life, Chullya. Wherever you go you will most definitely feel at One and in communion while traveling the ancient origins of the Andean Culture.

The Master Plant Teachers and Unity Consciousness

The intimate relationship between the human and plant world is one of profound nature. In all indigenous cultures, there are specific medicinal plants, whose constituents induce altered states and have an intense effect on the mind, the senses, and the spirit of man. The Master Plants, such as Ayahuasca, Huachuma and Peyote are viewed as Master Teachers and healers that contain within them the power to expand consciousness, reveal the truth of reality, activate dormant strands of DNA and reconnect one with their natural state of Oneness. The communion is experienced viscerally, in the body, not outside the body. The main reason I wish to bring the Master Plants into this conversation about Chullya is that they themselves are the universal wisdom keepers, shamans, guardians of the sacred, the curanderos and maestros whose frequencies reside and vibrate in Unity Consciousness. When ceremonially ingested, in the proper setting with an initiated and well-trained shaman, the master plants level of intelligence, their power to heal, and their ability to connect the one who has come to them, with the exact insight, shadow aspect or piece they need for healing is beyond measure. Not everyone is called to work with the plant teachers, nor is it the right path for everyone. However, combined with energy psychology, proper integration and shamanic counseling, these sacred ceremonies provide an opportunity to accelerate our healing and consciousness.

Pacha Mama's Message

As I sat in meditation at the base of the Pacha Mama Stone in Machu Picchu this is message that came through.

"It has been thousands of years since the children of earth have lived in tune with their Higher Nature - their Highest Light. Many of the children are desperately wanting to know their purpose - to reestablish connection with their High Self, but they don't believe in themselves and the power of their co-creative abilities. A rebirth is happening. A new cycle. Many of you are starting to awaken, but you are like little baby birds, pecking at the hard shell, the layers of illusion - layers of protection - and layers of false education. Just beginning to see the Light for the first time - Like the new born bird, your eyes are not yet ready to open. You are innocent and totally dependent on the safety and nurturing of your Mother. I too, am going through a rebirth and shaking free from the old structures. Create your sanctuaries and nests. Stay close to me. I will guide and hold you through this rebirth, until you are ready to fly."

It is true. Mankind has not lived in their higher nature for thousands of years. And so, it is a death and a rebirth, of magnificent proportions, that we experiencing during this current age. We are all on an epic journey of the Soul to return Home and reunite with the Divine Presence and our Luminous Essence. Our destiny is not a matter of chance, it is a matter of choice. Destiny is not to be waited for. It is to be pursued and achieved. This is a powerful time to reinstate Spiritual Law in your life, as the forces of the Upper World are infusing us all with new inspiration, clarity, passion, creativity and vision. Nothing is out reach. Ask how to get there and you will be shown the way. Allow the new designs of Light and the essence of The Golden Age to come through and inspire you, as life seeks its fullest and most glorious expression!

My prayer is that Love, Peace, Balance, Abundance, Liberation and Truth be made manifest for all Beings, through Divine Truth Light, the Cosmic Mother, and Eternal Child, as One, in whom we rest, abide and have our Being now and forever more.

In dedication to a future of beauty,

Chandra Sun Eagle

MOON
BOOKS

PAGANISM & SHAMANISM

What is Paganism? A religion, a spirituality, an alternative belief system, nature worship? You can find support for all these definitions (and many more) in dictionaries, encyclopaedias, and text books of religion, but subscribe to any one and the truth will evade you. Above all Paganism is a creative pursuit, an encounter with reality, an exploration of meaning and an expression of the soul. Druids, Heathens, Wiccans and others, all contribute their insights and literary riches to the Pagan tradition. Moon Books invites you to begin or to deepen your own encounter, right here, right now. If you have enjoyed this book, why not tell other readers by posting a review on your preferred book site.

Recent bestsellers from Moon Books are:

Journey to the Dark Goddess
How to Return to Your Soul
Jane Meredith
Discover the powerful secrets of the Dark Goddess and
transform your depression, grief and pain into healing
and integration.
Paperback: 978-1-84694-677-6 ebook: 978-1-78099-223-5

Shamanic Reiki
Expanded Ways of Working with Universal Life Force Energy
Llyn Roberts, Robert Levy
Shamanism and Reiki are each powerful ways of healing; together,
their power multiplies. *Shamanic Reiki* introduces techniques to
help healers and Reiki practitioners tap ancient healing wisdom.
Paperback: 978-1-84694-037-8 ebook: 978-1-84694-650-9

Pagan Portals – The Awen Alone
Walking the Path of the Solitary Druid
Joanna van der Hoeven
An introductory guide for the solitary Druid, *The Awen Alone* will
accompany you as you explore, and seek out your own place
within the natural world.
Paperback: 978-1-78279-547-6 ebook: 978-1-78279-546-9

A Kitchen Witch's World of Magical Herbs & Plants
Rachel Patterson
A journey into the magical world of herbs and plants, filled with
magical uses, folklore, history and practical magic. By popular
writer, blogger and kitchen witch, Tansy Firedragon.
Paperback: 978-1-78279-621-3 ebook: 978-1-78279-620-6

Medicine for the Soul
The Complete Book of Shamanic Healing
Ross Heaven
All you will ever need to know about shamanic healing and how to
become your own shaman...
Paperback: 978-1-78099-419-2 ebook: 978-1-78099-420-8

Shaman Pathways – The Druid Shaman
Exploring the Celtic Otherworld
Danu Forest
A practical guide to Celtic shamanism with exercises and
techniques as well as traditional lore for exploring the Celtic
Otherworld.
Paperback: 978-1-78099-615-8 ebook: 978-1-78099-616-5

Traditional Witchcraft for the Woods and Forests
A Witch's Guide to the Woodland with Guided Meditations and
Pathworking
Mélusine Draco
A Witch's guide to walking alone in the woods, with guided
meditations and pathworking.
Paperback: 978-1-84694-803-9 ebook: 978-1-84694-804-6

Naming the Goddess
Trevor Greenfield
Naming the Goddess is written by over eighty adherents and
scholars of Goddess and Goddess Spirituality.
Paperback: 978-1-78279-476-9 ebook: 978-1-78279-475-2

Shapeshifting into Higher Consciousness
Heal and Transform Yourself and Our World with Ancient
Shamanic and Modern Methods
Llyn Roberts
Ancient and modern methods that you can use every day to
transform yourself and make a positive difference in the world.
Paperback: 978-1-84694-843-5 ebook: 978-1-84694-844-2

Readers of ebooks can buy or view any of these bestsellers by
clicking on the live link in the title. Most titles are published in
paperback and as an ebook. Paperbacks are available in traditional
bookshops. Both print and ebook formats are available online.

Find more titles and sign up to our readers' newsletter at
http://www.johnhuntpublishing.com/paganism
Follow us on Facebook at https://www.facebook.com/MoonBooks
and Twitter at https://twitter.com/MoonBooksJHP

You may also like...

Ross Heaven
The Hummingbird's Journey to God
Perspectives on San Pedro; the Cactus of Vision

978-1-84694-242-6 (Paperback)
978-1-84694-638-7 (e-book)

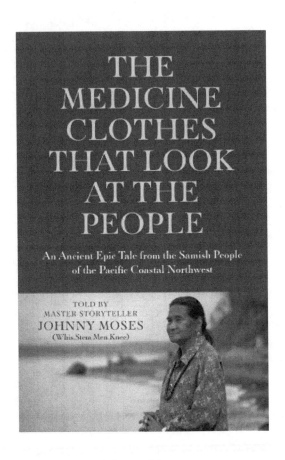

Johnny Moses

The Medicine Clothes that Look at the People

An Ancient Epic Tale from the Samish People of the Pacific Coastal Northwest

978-1-78904-395-2 (Paperback)
978-1-78904-396-9 (e-book)

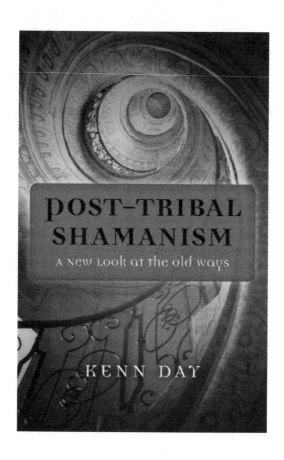

Kenn Day
Post-Tribal Shamanism
A New Look at the Old Ways

978-1-78099-619-6 (Paperback)
978-1-78099-620-2 (e-book)